TRUTH, MEANING AN[

26 / 4 / 2010

Dear Dad,

Happy philosophical birthday!

Love,
Adam
x x x

Truth, Meaning and Realism

A. C. GRAYLING

Professor of Philosophy,
Birkbeck College, London

continuum
LONDON • NEW YORK

Continuum UK
The Tower Building
11 York Road
London SE1 7NX

Continuum US
80 Maiden Lane
Suite 704
New York NY 10038

www.continuumbooks.com

First published 2007
First published in paperback 2008

British Library Cataloguing-in-Publication Data
A catalogue record for this book is available from the British Library.

ISBN: 978-1-8470-6154-6 (pb)

Typeset by Tony Lansbury, Tonbridge, Kent
Printed and bound in Great Britain by CPI Antony Rowe,
Chippenham, Wiltshire

Preface

There are three successively less ambitious outcomes that might be hoped for a philosophical argument: that it is watertight and therefore coerces the agreement of interlocutors; that it has some plausibility and therefore inclines interlocutors to consider whether it might be right; or finally that it is wrong in sufficiently interesting ways for it nevertheless to make a contribution to the topic in question, if only by suggesting alternative routes and possibilities. Modesty might be enough to make the second of these the summit of one's hopes, given the contests that rage over every millimetre of the conceptual terrain of philosophy; realism might choose the third.

Nevertheless, seeking to contribute to the conversation of philosophy is a worthy aspiration, and in the essays collected here I offer what are points of view, suggestions, *essais*, on the topics under discussion, and in no case take any of them to be remotely near a final word on the debates they relate to. It is for this reason relevant to mention that almost all these papers began as invited contributions to conferences, and a number have appeared in collections arising from those sources. This explains their exploratory character. Too many gifted colleagues publish too little for fear of not having every nut and bolt tightened into place; those who venture ideas as if they were letters to friends, trying out a way of thinking about something, and knowing that they will learn from the mistakes they make in doing so, do more both for the conversation and themselves thereby. The following pages contain endeavours very much of this latter kind.

Most of the technical philosophical work on which I have been engaged, in a career which has also involved a considerable commitment to applied and public aspects of philosophy, has focused on questions in the theory of knowledge, specifically the structure of justification underlying the capacity for epistemic agents such as ourselves to perceive and discourse about individuated aspects of the spatio-temporal domain. One might describe the target of enquiry there as the effort to describe the cognitive architecture of identifying thought. My more recent work published and unpublished on this topic will be collected into monograph form under the title *Scepticism and the Possibility of Knowledge* in due course. Working on those problems often and predictably required forays into the neighbouring fields of philosophical logic and the philosophies of language and mind. Here I bring together some of what I found compelling to discuss ancillary to the former enterprise in these directions.

The topics are truth, the nature of realism, aspects of meaning, concept reference, and the effect of fully intended clarity of expression in dissolving certain puzzles that might be artefacts of pragmatics rather than inherent problems of the logic of language. The point of addressing these questions becomes fully clear if one bears in mind that behind them lies a concern to understand how we think and talk about items and events in the world over which perceptual experience and ordinary language ranges. Without some sense of the complexities in these associated regions of enquiry, the task of understanding the relation of discourse to its domains remains incomplete.

I reprint here versions of two sections of the discussion of truth in my *Introduction to Philosophical Logic*. I do this because I should like to give the points they raise greater prominence, and because they bear directly on the discussion in others of the papers collected here. They concern treating '… is true' as a dummy predicate for more specific evaluatory predicates individuated by domains of discourse, and a challenge to Davidson's view that truth is indefinable. Also I change what, in its original published form, I called 'Perfect Speaker Theory' to 'Explicit Speaker Theory' in order to make more perspicuous the effort to suggest that *point* is the driving force in interpretation of implicatures by competent speakers of a natural language, and that this simple insight reveals certain familiar puzzles to be artefacts of inexplicitness. Original provenances are given in the footnotes to the individual chapters.

All the papers are of their time. Looking back at some of the earlier of them I am struck by how far the literature on each topic has accumulated, in some cases leaving the issues quite behind though they are by no means satisfactorily resolved. There are fashions and trends in philosophical interest, changes in which are frequently induced not by solutions and resolutions to problem areas, but by exhaustion of the resources and language for dealing with them. No doubt the text below that explores, for example, the realism-anti-realism question will at first seem to strike that note; but readers will see that I did not agree with the terms of the debate as it was then and still is commonly discussed, and that thus viewed its relevance to epistemological concerns remains direct and fresh. The same applies to the concept of truth and the nature of assertion; here too there is a requirement for ways of formulating conceptions of both (and their relation) that enrich understanding of the justificatory framework underlying quotidian epistemic practice. Such was my chief reason for addressing them, though in their own right they lie at the heart of much that matters in the collegial endeavour to achieve philosophical understanding overall. I collect them here, therefore, with due diffidence, as contributions to that task.

A. C. G.
BIRKBECK COLLEGE
UNIVERSITY OF LONDON
2007

Contents

1

Assertion, truth and evaluation

In what follows I offer an account of assertion that does not turn on a notion of truth reliant upon there being a distinction between the truth of what we say and think and there being grounds for saying and thinking as we do.[1] The importance of the question whether there can be such a theory is obvious: it is often taken as platitudinous that a notion of assertion (more generally, a notion of force) depends upon our having available just such a notion of truth. There has been discussion of whether the notion of truth involved in any *adequate* theory of assertion has to be 'substantial' or not, but, because the truth-involvingness of assertion is standardly taken for a platitude, there has been little discussion of whether a non-(realist)-truth-involving account is plausible. Even in the case where the order of dependence is held to run from assertion to truth – that is, in theories which say that understanding truth requires an antecedent understanding of assertion – there is an implication that the notions are correlative (perhaps that they 'essentially engage' with one another, in Crispin Wright's phrase). It may be right that an account of truth as a property of the content of assertions is parasitic on an account of the properties which might be ascribed to acts of assertion in evaluations of them – their appropriateness, relevance, correctness, and so forth – but if so that does not affect

---

1 A 'truth/grounds for truth' distinction is a distinction between an evidentially-unconstrained notion of truth of the kind standardly associated with 'realist' views, on the one hand, and on the other hand any view of truth (or warrant or verification) which is understood in essentially evidence-constrained ways. Abandoning the distinction may not force a truth-less treatment of assertion; but successfully providing a truth-less treatment fits well with certain reconstructions of the notion of truth of the kind suggested by its abandonment.

the suggestion being canvassed here, that assertion can be understood without reference to truth. I stress the point that by distinguishing between 'truth' and 'grounds for truth' I mean to mark, under the second heading, the relevant epistemically-constrained properties of contents: so 'truth' in what follows, unless qualified, is the familiar and standard non-epistemic realist notion.

Here is something that can be agreed as a datum: that ordinary discourse about the spatio-temporal world of things and events is straightforwardly realist in character. We think and talk as if our assertions are true or otherwise,[2] and true or otherwise in virtue of states of affairs which exist independently of our knowledge of them; which is in part to say, as if the referents of our expressions exist independently of our use of those expressions. This pretheoretical picture needs refinement, because the notion of 'independence' in play is too crude: we do better to think in terms of the relations between epistemic states of a discourser and the objective relata of his discourse, on this view describing the relations in question as external or contingent.

But this concerns the level of ordinary discourse. It is at the level of reflection[3] on ordinary discourse that the issue between 'realists' and their opponents is joined, in this way: the realist takes the commitments described as literally true, whereas his opponent denies this. Opposition to realism takes a diversity of forms, articulating in sometimes competing ways the grounds for denying realism's defining independence thesis (that is, its commitment to the independent existence of the targets of a given discourse from that discourse), thereby at least suggesting alter-

---

2 I don't think people are ordinarily committed to classical bivalence; they are (so to speak) informally two-valuing – true/not true – because they will allow the justice of saying of some statements that they fail to be true but not because they are false (perhaps because they are meaningless, or do not or cannot have either the value 'true' or the value 'false', as in cases of or like presuppositional failure).

3 If there were no risk of confusion (Alex Orenstein suggested to me there might be) I could distinguish the two levels as 'first-order' and 'second-order' on analogy with the distinction between the normative and metatheoretical levels at which moral discourse might be said to proceed. But merely a distinction of levels will do: most philosophy proceeds at the level of (more or less) detached reflection on some area of our thought or activity, and it is this level which I have in mind here.

native accounts of why first level discourse is or appears to be realist in character, and offering views about what should be said at the reflective level about the relation of discourse to what it ranges over. I am inclined to think that the diversity here is more apparent than otherwise, and arises from the fact that some of the formulations of why the realist claim is unsustainable are rather unhappy. But there are some genuine differences too. This is not the occasion for taxonomies, so I shall simply state what I take to be the best positive characterisation of a view that dispenses with realist commitments at the reflective level, by describing it as holding that those same commitments at the first level constitute undischargeable assumptions of discourse. The difference between the competing views so characterised is, despite initial appearances, large; quite different accounts of truth, objectivity, knowledge and possibility are prompted depending upon which is premised.[4]

This realism-opposing view belongs to a family of views some of which have been characterised as 'expressivist' in consequence of their resemblance to familiar theses in ethics and elsewhere.[5] This is not the thesis I urge here, as will emerge; but it is nevertheless worth stressing immediately that there is no suggestion in what I argue that we are *not really asserting* when we assert in the course of ordinary talk. More generally, there is no suggestion of some kind of error theory for what happens at the first level. No question arises about being wrong in one's realist assumptions if one is bound to make them, if there is genuinely no option to them: which is what the anti-realist just characterised holds.[6] All this is a matter for separate discussion, given elsewhere,[7] except for one crucial point: the realist's claim is that it is literally true that the spatio-temporal things we think and talk about exist

---

4 See my *Introduction to Philosophical Logoc*, chaps 8 and 9 and *passim*.

5 See Crispin Wright, 'Realism, Antirealism, Irrealism, Quasi-Realism' in P. A. French *et al.*, *Midwest Studies in Philosophy XII: Realism and Antirealism* (University of Minnesota Press, 1988), pp. 25 *et seq.*

6 By the same token, no question arises or can arise as to their truth or falsity: which is the short way with the realist who wishes to claim that they are literally true.

7 See my 'Epistemology and Realism', Proc. Arist. Soc. 1991–92; and 'On How Not To Be a Realist', below.

independently, in the sense explained of 'independent', of that discourse. Our conception of these things is therefore such for the realist that we can make sense of claims about their existence and character even when it lies beyond our epistemic competence to make, either directly or inferentially, their acquaintance. So, our discourse about these things does not rely for its meaning on epistemic constraints upon what can count as discourse about them, or upon the sense of expressions used in talk of them. This reflects the realist's view that the relation between discourse and its objects is external. In opposing this the anti-realist is stating that the relation is internal: that is, that any account of our discourse about the world must involve essential reference to the epistemic constraints governing its sense. (The pleonasm is there to insist on our taking the modality at face value.) Put more plainly still, the anti-realist holds that neither the meaning of what we say about the world nor, relatedly, our evaluation of what we say in terms of whatever turns out to be the evaluatory property of choice, can be uncontrolled by the availability of evidence for what we say and how we evaluate it. On the anti-realist view characterised here, and I think on any related view, this entails that there is no distinction to be drawn between the truth of whatever the truth-bearers are, and there being grounds for someone to hold them true.

But can there be an adequate theory of assertion on this view? Assertion is one of the most central and basic activities of our discourse, and the need to understand it is crucial. A problem as to whether the present kind of anti-realist can have an adequate theory of assertion seems to arise, as noted, because of the supposed fact that there is no giving an account of force in general and assertion in particular unless we have available an adequate truth/grounds distinction, that is, a distinction aimed at preserving a notion of truth which cannot be collapsed into something essentially evidence-constrained. According to those who hold that assertion can only be understood in such terms, the role of an uncollapsable notion of truth is central because normative: they take it that for a substantial constraint on the practice of assertion there has to be a requirement that assertion 'aims at' truth, so they cannot be satisfied if the asserter's having grounds for taking what he asserts to be true is all that is available.

Therefore truth-value must be a property which attaches to the content of assertions independently of anyone's reasons for predicating it of them.[8]

This is what gives weight to the 'platitude' that assertion is essentially truth-involving. Here are two examples of its statement. John McDowell writes: 'Now there is a truistic connection between the content of an assertion and a familiar notion of truth ... the connection guarantees, as the merest platitude, that a correct specification of what can be asserted, by the assertoric utterance of a sentence, cannot but be a specification of a condition under which the sentence is true.' Crispin Wright likewise takes it to be platitudinous that 'an assertion is a claim that something is true';[9] that 'to assert a statement is to present it as true';[10] that 'the notion of truth essentially engages with that of assertion';[11] and that 'assertoric discourse is aimed at truth'.[12]

Wright criticises fellow anti-realists who try to reinterpret assertoric accounts of certain areas of discourse so that the assertions we make or appear to make while engaged in them do not involve realist commitments. The reinterpretation involves treating the utterances in question not as claims about items in an independent realm of facts, but as expressions of the utterer's attitudes; 'expression' indeed *replaces* 'assertion', as in certain well-known versions of ethical anti-realism.[13] Wright takes it that expressivists would agree that to assert 'is to make a claim about reality',[14] which is what prompts them to reinterpret, for they are bound on this view to hold that whatever does not make a claim about reality had better not be an assertion, that is, had better not be a laying claim to truth.

In Wright's view, it is not just that the objections to expressivism are overwhelming, but that the thrust of the expressivist

---

8 *Cf.* Crispin Wright, *ibid.*, p. 36.

9 *Ibid.*, p. 32.

10 *Ibid.*, p. 34 and again, p. 35.

11 *Ibid.*, p. 35; this can be true on the reverse view, that it is in terms of the properties of assertion (correctness, etc.) that truth is to be understood, as, for example, Dummett has it.

12 *Ibid.*

13 *Ibid.*, p. 30.

14 *Ibid.*

view is misdirected. He says that instead of attempting to recon-strue assertoric discourse as something else, that is, as non-truth-aimed discourse, anti-realists should leave assertion's link with truth alone, and instead seek to decouple it from realism. The assertion-truth link is to be maintained by understanding truth in the thinnest possible way consistent with its still provid-ing a substantial constraint on assertoric practice – a normativity constraint – and with its property of exercising 'rational com-mand' still intact, 'rational command' being the hold truth has over those who, 'appropriately endowed', make appropriate use of that endowment.[15]

This is where the remarks in the opening paragraphs above become relevant. To assert something is of course to say some-thing about reality; but 'reality' is not the bone of contention between realists and anti-realists; rather, their dispute concerns the *relation* of discourse to reality, in particular, the question whether that relation is external or internal. The realist states his view that it is external in terms of an insistence on the distinction between truth and grounds for truth; his opponent's view that it is internal consists in a collapsing of the distinction. A collapse of the distinction is equivalent to replacing the notion of truth with an epistemic notion. Therefore, any decoupling of assertion from either one of realism or truth is on the present view a decoupling from both: and therefore again, a notion of assertion which is not merely a claim that our assertoric practice at the first level is really something else, is going to have to be an account of that practice which is both adequate in itself and at the same time shrived of an appeal to a notion of truth in the realist's sense (that is, truth under the independence thesis). Accordingly, the account to follow does not adopt Wright's strategy of seeking a notion of truth suitable to a theory of assertion which is nevertheless decoupled from realism. Among Wright's chief reasons for wishing to find such a notion of truth are those relating to the normativity and 'rational command' points: it is a test of the

---

15 *Ibid.*, p. 37. Is there is a possibility of circularity in this notion, so charac-terised? Perhaps there is a problem with the 'appropriates'. Since I am not defending an expressivist thesis I shall not here pursue Wright's further points on substantiality in a notion of truth.

adequacy of the account to follow that it can respect both without appeal even to the thinnest notion of truth capable of providing them.

One thing which needs to be stated straight away is that it is potentially misleading, and therefore I shall avoid it, to try to characterise assertion either as 'fact stating discourse' or as 'saying that'. The reasons, briefly, are as follows.

If one thinks of assertion as 'fact stating discourse', as Strawson and Huw Price do,[16] one runs the risk of begging the question, because it seems hard to envisage an account of facts which is not already truth-involving, where truth is a substantial notion. It is indeed surprising that the *per obscuris* nature of the appeal to facts in accounts of assertion has not long since been taken as a reason for avoiding it.

An oddity attaches to characterising assertion as 'fact stating discourse' even on the view that truth and assertion are essentially related, for the reason that it is clear that there can be false assertions, which *ipso facto* do not state facts. So even on this view fact stating is, at best, what only true assertions succeed in doing; and if the stating of facts is to figure centrally in an account of assertion, it would therefore have to be as what the asserter intends to do, not as what in fact he does. He in fact does this only when certain further conditions – specifically, conditions of success – have been fulfilled, and explaining these will be just where a notion of truth is bound to enter; so, in connection either with the explanation of the nature of facts, or with evaluation of what counts as reports of them, a perhaps substantial notion of truth looks to be essentially in the offing. Either way, therefore, to construe assertion as 'fact stating discourse' begs the question.

The problem with treating assertion as 'saying that', which we naturally do in thinking about reported assertions and other indirect contexts, is that 'saying that' seems to denote a class of utterances of which assertion is just one member. This is illustrated by the cases of deceiving and lying, in which someone says that p in order to mislead an audience, and hence is not asserting p,

---

16 Strawson, P. F., 'Truth' in *Logico-Linguistic Papers* (London, 1971); Price, H., 'Truth and the Nature of Assertion' in *Mind*, Vol. 86, No. 382, pp. 202–220; and *Facts and the Function of Truth* (Oxford, 1988), esp. pp. 9–13.

because he does not believe that p; indeed his disbelieving p is a condition of his deceiving or lying to his audience. It is natural to gloss what occurs as his pretending to assert p, for he intends that his audience should take it that he is asserting p; and this is just what is happening. But if he is pretending to assert p, then he is not asserting p. Still, he is saying that p. So there are cases of saying that which are not cases of assertion. It is worth keeping this distinction in mind because it might be that there are properties of sayings-that which it is better not to ascribe to assertions.

An objector might at this juncture be tempted to say that drawing the asserting/saying-that distinction in this way positively cries out for a notion of truth, since what the deceiver wishes to do is to get his audience to believe something to be true which he believes to be false; and it is because what the deceiver says is false that he is not asserting p but only appearing to assert it: thus demonstrating the very interdependence of truth and assertion here being rejected. It will be another test of the adequacy of the account here ventured that it shows that we need not yield to this temptation.

My analysis of assertion has it that assertion is expression of a complex attitude, an attitude constitutive of S's conceptual commitments, S's having which – and in this way – puts them into a disciplined relation of engagement with responsible belief and action elsewhere in S's epistemic concerns, and more broadly with his commitments to his epistemic community. (The apparent handsome begging of the question in the account now given is addressed after the sketch.) When S asserts p, S is doing the following things: S is expressing a belief that p, and correlatively a preparedness to act on p if that is relevant. S is accordingly marking commitment to an epistemic evaluation of p which places it higher than competitors q, r to p, and expressing that commitment. S is also thereby marking p as a proper and, at least on the occasion of assertion, relevant component in a description or account of some state of affairs, or at least as relevant to public evaluation of the subject-matter in a given stretch of discourse. (People may assert things when solitary, but standardly their *point* is given by their place in a communication context.) S's commitments in the above respects consist in his regarding p as a licence to infer q, r, and so on; in the standard case, by serving as a premise in such an inference. (There are other direct and less direct ways in which p can be an inference-licenser for derivations of some r from q, q', etc: as a covering law licensing a range of particular inferences, or as a statement of conceptual policy: more on this emerges shortly.) In the standard communication setting for assertion, S's commitments in the above respects further commit him to enjoining interlocutors to make the same commitments: this is the prescriptive element noted by Carnap. Consensus in the right degree at the right level is vital to communication, and so what is going to count as 'the facts' – thinly understood as whatever endorsed propositions report – must be established between interlocutors. Accordingly, acts of assertion – which are acts among these other things of *proposing* (advancing propositions) – are ways of negotiating the framework of discussion, because by their nature they invite agreement or disagreement, and where either is principled and motivated, and therefore comes supported by reasons making claims to our rational respect, there will be, broadly speaking, one of three outcomes: the original assertion will be permitted to stand, or it will be replaced by an agreed alternative, or it will be dropped. So assertion has the function of keying a region of discourse: it provides the assumptions to be held firm, and makes room for certain moves in the region – again, for the central example, inference – while blocking certain others and showing where the region's boundaries might lie. Take a simple example: someone says, 'your cup of tea is on the conservatory table'. Whether that assertion is accepted or disputed, the approximate range of things that can be said about, for example, the whereabouts of the cup of tea has been suggested, and a bundle of immediate inferences settled. (Suppose one accepts that the cup of tea is on the conservatory table. Then one cannot assert that the same cup of tea is simultaneously on the conservatory floor. And so on.)

This account is in a sense 'expressivist', and at the same time functionalist. It is not expressivist in Wright's sense, for it does not seek to replace assertion construed as truth-aimed with expression construed as in the familiar examples: for one such, as manifesting a subjective state of belief (and such states can be arbitrary). Rather, it is an expression of something constrained: a cognitive attitude carrying commitments to believing and acting in further constrained ways, keyed by the attitude to the content which asserting it expresses. The functional aspect of this lies in these connections: in the obligations to further belief, inference and action, and their place in the publicly shared nexus of belief, inferential possibilities and action to which the asserter commits himself by his assertion. Because asserting has these immediate consequences for the asserter – and, if they accept it, his audience – in the cognitive and practical domains, it has to lie under government of tough normative constraints, which include specification of tests for the right kinds of links between assertions and their grounds, for the adequacy of the grounds, and for the relevance of acts of assertion to the circumstances of their making.

One way of pointing up the contrast which analysing assertion in terms of such commitments makes with analysing it in terms of truth, is to say that what assertion has as its aim is not the presentation of or laying claim to truth, but the realisation of certain cognitive and practical goals: grounding inferences and representing a segment of the world as being fit for certain thoughts about it and actions respecting it.

What was given above is not a list of *alternative* things S is doing when S asserts p, but the complex of things which assertion consists in. Each of its aspects invites comment, and I offer some shortly. First, however, I deal with the obvious objection.

The obvious objection is that this way of characterising assertion, far from proceeding without recourse to a notion of truth, simply paraphrases the *term* 'truth' away, but does not dispense with the concept. Surely, the objector will say, the question-begging nature of this account manifests itself when one points out that 'S believes p' means 'S believes that p is true', and 'S enjoins interlocutors to share his commitment to p' means 'S advises or instructs or urges interlocutors to take p to be true too', and so on for the other formulations. In short, what S is committing himself to in asserting p is just: the truth of p.

There are two independent responses, the second of which is stronger. The first is a familiar one. It is to ask, what does it add to 'S believes p' to tack on 'is true'? Does 'S believes p to be true' say something else or something more than 'S believes p'? Now, this redundancy charge is not effective across the board, because there are plenty of cases, individuated by context, where something can indeed be added by adding 'is true': endorsement and emphasis at the rhetorical level, prescription or persuasion at the strategic level, the marking of various kinds of imprimatur for epistemic purposes, perhaps of the very kinds connoted by the talk just now of forging agreements over the framework for some region of discourse. At the level of ordinary talk, employment of the predicate introduces a useful shorthand for these purposes. But note that use of a convenient phraseology to mark the performance of these acts of prescribing or reaching framework agreements entails nothing further: what is added in these cases by talk of truth can, in the first place, be added by talk of other things (the examples just given), which means that reference to truth can be eliminated in favour of more precise evaluatory notions, and in the second place, however it is added, it is *added*, that is, it is not essential to the analysis of assertion. So when one says that S's asserting p expresses S's belief that p, we add nothing by adding 'is true' (and so for the other cases). Here, therefore, the charge of redundancy is appropriate. In recognising this, we recognise that what S is committed to in asserting p is not the truth of p, but the consequences of asserting p: the consequences of seeing matters in a certain way, drawing certain inferences therefore, and acting in accordance with both.

A point that might be urged at this juncture against the redundancy defence is that predicating truth of utterances indeed does something; it introduces the substantive constraint, mentioned earlier, that a concept of truth imposes because of its requirement that asserters should have a better call on our epistemic respect than can be provided by their own unsupplemented doxastic states alone. This is a valuable reminder, because here the response is to point out that to assert is always to imply possession of grounds for the assertion; and what it is to have grounds for an assertion is a demanding matter, because the linguistic community – which has to take assertion seriously – is intolerant of too many irresponsible calls on its attention (pretended assertion cries wolf). So, there are austere normative tests of adequacy for the making of assertions, their severity proportional to their importance in cognitive and practical transactions. They are to be made out wholly in terms of the possession of grounds and the relation between grounds and the assertions they justify, based on critically reflective evaluatory standards for dealing with the 'error, ignorance, and [the need for] improved assessment' which count among the crucial concerns of epistemic practice.[17]

There is a case for saying not just that we add nothing in adding 'is true', but that we may well be misleading ourselves, for reasons implicit in the second response, which is this: arguably, the formulations given of what S does in asserting p come centrally down to the related matters of S's giving a higher epistemic valuation to p than to its competitors, his treating it as licensing inferences to q, r etc; and his being prepared, in relevant cases, to act on it. In nothing of this is a notion of truth concerned. One way of illustrating this is to imagine some game-theoretic structure where relative evaluation of items determines which further moves are required, permitted, or prudent in the light of some goal. The idea of a conceptual framework, mooted earlier, is the natural domicile for an account of assertion made out in these terms. Moreover, it closely models what happens in the course of epistemic life, which is always lived and calculated from the agent perspective, and not (except perhaps in retrospect) from an idealised external vantage-point where the agent's calculations can be assessed for the degree to which they succeed in discovering to him some part of a range of otherwise hidden facts.

The defence here can be put more simply and generally by taking the example of any game in which role-players communicate to each other information relevant to the evolution of the game towards the goal of winning it. So, for example, imagine two teams playing an online version of a war-game, the winners being the team with more 'survivors' at the end of a given time period. Team members will make assertions about states of affairs in the virtual world of the game, inform one another, equip one another with premises from which inferences can be drawn, and so on, just as if the world of the game were not virtual but real; but with

---

17 *Cf.* Wright, *ibid.,* p. 36. Wright allows that the call for a 'proper pedigree for assertion' with proper grounds for criticism of it is by no means a call for too much. I agree; it is in particular not a call for truth, although Wright goes on immediately to suggest that truth is part of the package that the pedigree and the criticism constitute.

no assumption that any of the claims made and information given is anything other than, in effect, moves in an inferential set. The obvious remark here is that their assertions are 'just as if true', and a closely similar analysis of virtual truth can be given as of fictional truth. But this misses the point about the cognitive attitudes to be ascribed to the players in asserting that things are thus-and-so in the virtual domain of the game: it is misleading to say that they take their assertions to be 'true in the game though not literally true', as if a refined and adapted notion of truth in different domains were required to make sense of the point of their asserting what they do. Rather, it is more accurate to say that they take their assertions to be relevant, informative, and inference-guiding in the context. And now a different thought supervenes: that it is easy and economical to wrap this character-isation into the claim that they take their assertions to be true, but note this: that this constitutes an account of truth for the context, rather than being an invocation of the notion of truth as primitive to and therefore explanatory of the context. This would be a reason for thinking that assertion explains truth, but if so, truth cannot be invoked to explain assertion, and certainly not on the basis of a distinction between truth and possession of grounds for taking an utterance or belief to be true.

The comments invited by this sketch of an analysis of assertion are heterogeneous, and I offer just some. First, it is notable that in some discussions of assertion, for example Huw Price's, the idea that 'S asserts p' is in part to be analysed as 'S expresses a belief that p' is dismissed on the grounds that it involves an unaccept-able psychologism. There seems to be a need for a distinction here, between cases where S reports his personal doxastic incli-nations, and cases where he offers p to interlocutors as something that they can and should incorporate into their body of beliefs because (at least, but standardly among other things, e.g. its being relevant to the circumstances) it meets the austere critical stan-dards applied by the linguistic community whenever the serious business of assertion is in hand. The difference lies in the intended effect of the communication. A report on one's personal views, and an attempt to communicate to others items of relevance in some shared context of discourse, may indeed coincide: but the linguistic community is not without resource in distinguishing the two when they do not coincide, in particular when a statement of a personal conviction on some matter is offered as no more than that.

But there is not too much mileage for an objector in the claim that when S asserts p S is thereby expressing a belief that p, for it is hardly surprising that this should be a component of the complex act being performed. It is a necessary condition of S's asserting p that S believes p; if S did not believe p, then even if he utters a sentence that could otherwise be used to assert p, he cannot be asserting it. This much is plain from the point about holding apart the notions of assertion and saying-that in the way explained earlier, and demonstrates the need for doing so.

The concept of 'epistemic evaluation', made out in terms of preferring assertion of certain contents over others, need not detain us long either. The natural suggestion is to think in terms of measures for adjusting our epistemic judgments to the available evidence, and there are obviously ways of doing this which do not require that we mutually involve the notions of probability and truth. There is a natural and attractive inclination to think that assignments of probabilities are just ways of calibrating our confidence in the truth of some claim; even to treat truth and falsity as the limiting cases for the scale used in matching evidence to expectation. But there is in fact no pressure to insert 'the truth of' into that attractive statement, and especially not to interpret the discourse-neutral concept of epistemic evaluation in terms of truth,[18] still less to think that there is no way of doing otherwise. Once again, the idea of having refined techniques of assessment for the adequacy of grounds for assertions is not essentially truth-involving, which is the point of insistence here.

In the account given it is taken to be central to assertion that the act constitutes a complex commitment to giving its content a certain place in a tree of inferences and actions whose branchings it therefore helps to determine. A feature of treating assertion as such a commitment is that it permits reading some of what S holds as (so to speak) his stock of assertible contents from the

---

18 *Cf.* chapters 4 and 5 on '_is true' as 'lazy' for specific predicates of evaluation, individuated by discourse.

way the network of his inferences and actions has branched, just
as one can, in the opposite direction, do what S intends one to do
on the basis of his assertions, namely predict the branchings they
determine. Since one component of S's asserting p is that it
expresses his belief that p, this permits the kinds of interpretation
of his discourse, and the explanation of his behaviour, which
some accounts make central respectively to linguistic understanding and a theory of action. The two-way traceability is
informative in the more general sense that it shows assertion's
engagement with other dimensions of practice. A way of illustrating the connection is to compare it to a punter's readiness to
lay a bet on the basis of his assessment of odds. The difference
between betting on horses and asserting is that since the asserter
is also committed, in relevant circumstances, to enjoining others
to lay the same bet, a more critically refined test for the appropriateness of the assertion has to be implied as met: which is
where epistemic evaluation and acceptance of its consequences
immediately mesh. The tests have to be such that anyone well
enough placed to run them would have to be coerced by their
outcomes into according them the kind of epistemic valuation
which others in his linguistic community would agree is appropriate (which they, in those circumstances, would be coerced to
accord likewise): this marks the place where a substantial constraint on assertion bears. A full account would address the
two concerns drawn earlier from Wright's demands on the notion
of truth he identifies as required for explaining assertion: the
regulative requirement that asserters meet their audience's expectations in having good enough grounds for making an assertion,
and the agreement over the adequacy of the grounds which results
in some content's being rated 'assertible' by any standardly competent member of the linguistic community who is suitably placed
to make the assessment.

These ideas might be made out more fully in terms of the
framework of inference as a whole, and how by means of the
practice of assertion and challenge – which is in short to say,
debate – it is negotiated.[19] It is here that the concepts of infer-

---

19 See my 'Epistemic Finitude and the Framework of Inference', in *Scepticism
and the Possibility of Knowledge,* forthcoming.

ence-licensing and 'conceptual policy' take centre stage, and help to articulate the idea that the realistic features of our discourse at the ordinary level constitute undischargeable assumptions of the scheme. That is another story: for present purposes one suggestion it prompts merits remark. Assertion is an operation on its content: so much is common ground, for the dispute concerns primarily how to specify the nature of the operation being performed. As remarked earlier it is fruitful to ponder the relation between the properties ascribed to acts of assertion in evaluations of them, such as correctness, appropriateness and relevance, and the notions both of sense and of the other forces. The suggestion is this. Assertions are evaluated in terms of the evidence that prompts them. There is a smooth way of connecting that fact with thoughts about what a speaker knows who knows the senses of expressions used in making those assertions, namely, by exploiting the idea that evaluatory conditions for assertion specify sense. Again, it might be proposed that assertion is the 'radical' force (the root or basic force), in the sense that the other forces are to be understood in terms of it: thus, interrogation and ordering are construed as parasitic on the operation or potential operation of assertion in familiar ways: interrogation is the act of enquiring whether, ordering the act of commanding that, some p is assertible.

If someone were to flesh out this suggestion, the effect of which is to place assertion at the centre of theories of discourse, it would be of particular importance to notice the link between assertion and judgment, the supremely epistemic act. When Ramsey recommended a shift of attention away from truth in this area of enquiry, the place to which he thought we should shift it is precisely there.

I conclude by remarking that one can of course discuss whether or not assertion essentially involves truth independently of concerns about realism. My reason for linking the question of assertion to the realism dispute is, as noted earlier, that certain realism-opposing concerns appear to be subverted if we cannot give an account of assertion that dispenses with appeal to truth realistically understood. But this suggests another motivation: the combination of the obscurity of a realist notion of truth, and the importance of the notion of assertion, surely invite a search for an account of the latter that does without the former.

2

Metaphysically innocent representation

What follows attempts the strategic task of showing that a certain familiar debate in contemporary philosophy benefits from being recast in a way which, although on the face of it appearing more traditional than its current form, provides a means of getting its essentials right. The debate is the central and ancient one about the relation of mental and linguistic states and activities, on the one hand, to their targets – for present purposes, in the spatio-temporal domain – on the other hand. It is now standardly described as a debate about realism for the domain in question. The mental and linguistic states and activities at issue variously comprise perceiving, referring to, thinking and theorising about, saying something true of, and the like.

As a peg to hang the following thoughts on I begin with two views to the effect that there can be metaphysically innocent representation, that is, representation, or referential content, and like states of subjects, which is not ontologically committal or assumptive in characteristically realist ways. The two views are close enough to have interesting differences, and to be arguably wrong in interestingly similar ways; and it is these points I wish to draw out. The views are respectively associated with contemporary philosophers who give them distinctive and easily recognisable forms, namely, Putnam and Rorty. I do not aim to engage in exegesis or criticism of their views, but will concentrate on statements of their positions which, whether or not they coincide exactly with their originals, give us the core of the problem.[1]

---

1 I quote *ad libitem* in the first part of what follows from Putnam, H., *Realism with a Human Face* (Harvard, 1990) and *Words and Life* (Harvard, 1992) and from Rorty, R., *Consequences of Pragmatism* (Minneapolis, 1982), "Putnam and the Relativist Menace" in *Journal of Philosophy*, September 1993, and "Reply to Putnam" in *Rorty And His Critics* (ed. R. Brandon) (Oxford, 2000).

On Rorty's view, the very idea of representation loses content when we recognise the force of the question: How can we say that statements are made true by things in the world if those things are not independent of our ways of talking about them? Rorty takes Putnam to be an ally because Putnam argues that 'it makes no sense to think of the world as dividing itself up into "objects" (or "entities") independently of our use of language. It is *we* who divide up "the world" – that is, the events, states of affairs and physical, social, etc., systems that we talk about – into "objects", "properties" and "relations", and we do this in a variety of ways.' A simple example is that we think of the contents of a room, say, either as furniture or as collections of elementary particles, depending on our interests and purposes. A corollary of this view is that different ontologies can be adopted for the same states of affairs, which means that apparently inconsistent pairs of statements can both be true, in the sense of being true 'in the way of speaking to which each belongs' (so the inconsistency is *only* apparent). Putnam calls this 'conceptual relativity'.

Putnam's response to Rorty's use of this insight is to repudiate the assumptions that underlie not just the dichotomy but Rorty's reliance on the dichotomy in stating his own refusal to think in terms of it. (Putnam regards Rorty as being trapped in the terms – specifically metaphysical – which the dichotomy imposes.) The idea of the 'independent existence' of objects from talk of them employs notions of causal or logical independence that are not, Putnam claims, ordinary ones; when we use 'independent' ordinarily ('in the only way I can understand', as he puts it) there is no question but that the blueness of the sky is independent of the way we talk. So we can retain a notion of representation made intelligible by Putnam's 'conceptual relativism', the view that there are different descriptions of the same state of affairs, that is, different ontologies we can adopt for them. On this conception, we can talk of referring to objects, but not in the same metaphysically privileged way, for there is a variety of ways of doing so: this recalls Putnam's 'model theoretic' argument: 'we can think of our words and thoughts as having determinate reference to objects (when it is clear what sort of "objects" we are talking about and what vocabulary we are using); but there is no fixed sense of "reference" involved.' This shows that rejection of metaphysical realism does not entail the collapse of the notion of representation, nor does it promote the sense of a certain *confinement* – being trapped inside language or thought – which Putnam's earlier position had to some extent helped to foster.

Putnam thinks these considerations offer a metaphysically innocent way of taking it that thoughts are *about* the world, that language *represents* the world, that our beliefs are *justified* by how the world is, because they recover the ordinary, 'humble' sense of such words as 'represent', 'justified', thought', 'world'. He quotes Wittgenstein with approval: 'if the words "language", "experience", "world" have a use, it must be as humble a one as that of the words "table", "lamp", "door".'

Now, I wish to agree with this, as far as it goes. But it does not seem to go far enough, because it leaves out a vital extra step in the diagnosis of the problem with the view both Putnam and Rorty agree in repudiating (*viz.* the strong standard view that the relata in mind-world relations are independent of one another), and therefore does not make explicit what kind of relations the metaphysically innocent mind-world relations are. To see this one needs to address directly the question of what is at stake in the debate about realism. The claim I pursue, taking a route different from Putnam's, is that it is a mistake to cast matters in metaphysical terms at all. From this mischoice of key flow the mischiefs of the debate. What one should recognise instead is that the crucial points are entirely epistemological. Once transposed to this key – where much of the advance in our understanding of these problems was first made in modern philosophy, so this a retransposition, taking us to the status quo ante Dummett's Frege – we see how to resist the threat implicit in extreme forms of post-modern, relativistic, rationality-free anti-realisms not unlike Rorty's.

There is a definite conclusion to be drawn once the retuning is complete: which is that although there are indeed metaphysically innocent representations, there are no epistemically innocent ones.

To keep matters clear let us remember that the motivation in this region is to escape what some see as a fundamental problem generated by the Cartesian tradition, namely, the premising of a mind-world divide. Questions about the dichotomy, and therefore the relation of mental to physical phenomena, takes many more forms than its original manifestation as the mind-body problem and the question of scepticism as conceived in standard epistemology. With its deepening and nuancing, the debate has, familiarly, come to focus upon truth, reference, and realistic understandings of both. The solution adopted by some (identified by Rorty as Dewey, Heidegger and Wittgenstein) and in various ways by others, is to repudiate the divide they see as the source of the problem: the divide between the representing, thinking, referring, perceiving, experiencing, discoursing mind, and what it represents, thinks or discourses about, refers to, or perceives. Realism – 'metaphysical realism' in Putnam's terminology – is taken to be *the* commitment to the existence of this divide. But giving up the divide is not – at least in the views of Putnam and Davidson; Rorty thinks differently – to opt for a strong form of anti-realism, perhaps of the kind that might be a natural corollary of idealism. But as with the later work of Wittgenstein, it is not entirely clear what the non-anti-realistic anti-realism of these writers comes to. They retreat into such claims as that we can help ourselves to philosophically unproblematic, deflated sense of 'truth' and 'reference'; or that there are ordinary, 'humble' uses of 'represent', 'justify' and the like, that only seem philosophically problematic because philosophers wilfully make them so; that everything is all right with our concepts, just as they seem to be when we are sufficiently unreflective about them.

But for both the ordinary language-user and the unreconstructed non-Wittgensteinian philosopher, it seems that thinking in terms of the repudiated divide is both apt and powerful; and to the latter at least the divide can sometimes seem *interestingly* problematic, which is to say, in ways that promise to tell us much about both mind and world. And this is because the mind-world relations are not independent of one another – far from it – as reflection on the following (redundant) list implies:

(1) perceiving (or 'experiencing); which involves applying concepts, and therefore (at least rudimentary, perhaps 'folk') theory; both of which are implicated in all the following;

(2) referring to (picking out, individuating, identifying items in or portions of the world);

(3) intending ('the directedness of consciousness');

(4) predicating of (describing, qualifying, modifying); saying (attempting to say) something true of (asserting, and the phrastic components of utterances of other forces);

(5) representing (thinking about/having thoughts about theorising about); informally, in folk physics and folk psychology, as required above (sometimes described as 'having a conceptual scheme'); formally, in the natural and social sciences;

(6) having beliefs about, knowing/having knowledge of (under the tightest constraints on 'to know'; chiefly, that the truth condition is satisfied);

and so on. There is much to be said about these relations and the relations between them, most of which is a task for another place and time. Here I shall be selective in pursuit of the claim that the debate about metaphysically non-committal representation turns essentially on epistemic concerns, focusing especially on the claim that whatever else might be said about these relations, they are not 'independence' relations.

Part of the argument is that this is recognised by the debate's major players: both Putnam and Dummett identify as definitive of realism the claim that truth is radically non-epistemic, that is, that what we say and think and what we speak of or think about are independent of one another. Nevertheless Putnam continues to describe realism as a metaphysical thesis, Dummett as a semantic one. Yet neither could be more explicit in characterising it in epistemic terms.

Dummett says that a realistic conception of statements in some class turns on the idea that their truth-values are settled by knowledge-independent states of affairs. I give two representative quotations: 'The very minimum that realism can be held to involve is that statements in the given class relate to some reality that exists *independently of our knowledge of it*, in such a way that reality renders each statement in the class determinately true or false, *again independently of whether we know, or are even able to discover, its truth-value*.[2] [T]he fundamental thesis of

---

2 Dummett, M. A. E., 'Realism', *Synthese* 52 (1982), p. 55 – references henceforth 'RS'.

realism, so regarded, is that we really do succeed in referring to external objects, existing independently of our knowledge of them, and that the statements we make about them are rendered true or false by an objective reality the constitution of which is, again, *independent of our knowledge*.'[3]

You will recall that Dummett's reason for characterising realism as a thesis about truth rather than ontology is that 'certain kinds of realism, for instance realism about the future or about ethics, do not seem readily classifiable as doctrines about realms of entities'.[4] This recognises that metaphysics is not the crucial concern; but it looks past Dummett's own epistemic characterisation of the central realistic commitment to a consequence for semantics consistent with it, and perhaps naturally a corollary of it, but not entailed by it.

Metaphysical realism is described by Putnam as the thesis that the world consists of mind-independent objects. In fact he describes the commitment more strongly, as the view that the world consists of a fixed totality of mind-independent objects. And he argues that one who holds this takes it to follow that there is exactly one true and complete description of the world, and that therefore truth consists in a form of correspondence between it and that description. Perhaps partly under the influence of Dummett's ways of characterising realism, Putnam puts these points alternatively as the view that metaphysical realism is a set of theses about truth, namely 'that truth is a matter of Correspondence and that it exhibits Independence (of what humans do or could find out), Bivalence, and Uniqueness (there cannot be more than one true or complete description of Reality)'.[5]

In Putnam's terminology, the property – 'Independence' – that distinguishes realistically-conceived truth is its 'radically non-epistemic' character (*cf.* Frege's sharp distinction between truth and grounds for truth); the claim that truth is Independent is the claim that 'the world could be such that the theory we are most

---

3 RS, p. 104. See also *The Logical Basis of Metaphysics* (1991) (henceforth LBM), pp. 9, 345, my emphases.
4 RS, p. 55, LBM, chap. 1, *passim*, 'Realism' TOE, *passim*.
5 *Representation and Reality* (MIT Press, 1989), p. 107.

justified in accepting would not really be true ... rational acceptability is one thing, truth is another'.[6]

These ways of characterising realism show that the confusion
infecting the debate about it arises from conflating two ways of
thinking about 'independence'. The first way is familiar in its
different guises as a metaphysical commitment, historically
expressed as commitment to some notion of substance; but it
is not easy to state precisely. It consists in describing the entities
in a given realm as existing in their own right, independently
of other things which cause or, less strongly, in some way keep
them in being (subvene them, perhaps). Such existents might
be thought of as having the status of Aristotle's 'primary being',
or as substances conceived as those things which exist, and can
only be understood as existing, in some sense 'in and of themselves'. If anything merited the label 'metaphysical realism', this
would be it. This ontological understanding of independence is,
familiarly, well despatched by Putnam's arguments.

The second sense of 'independence', and the one genuinely at
issue in the debate, as both Putnam and Dummett show, is *epistemic independence*. Someone applies such a notion if he holds
that the entities in some realm exist *independently of any
thought, talk, knowledge or experience of them*. The realist and
the anti-realist do not dispute the existence or otherwise of the
entities; they agree that they exist; what they dispute is the manner in which the entities are related to cognition of them. Often
this thesis is expressed in terms of the 'mind-independence' of the
given entities. When those who discuss realism (thus *epistemically*
conceived) mistakenly contrast it with the (*metaphysical* thesis
of) idealism, it is clear that they have mind-independence in mind
as its chief characteristic.

More circumstantially put, realism states that the knowledge
relation is external, contingent and limited; it states (a) that the
objects of which we seek knowledge can and for the most part do lie
outside our powers of access to them, and (b) that the sense of
remarks about the existence and character of these entities or realms
is not governed by considerations relating to our epistemic powers.

---

6 'Model Theory and the Factuality of Semantics' in *Reflections on Chomsky*,
George, A. (ed.), (Blackwell, 1989), p. 214.

In the anti-realist considerations advanced by Dummett it is the incoherence of (b) which serves as the primary focus. That offers an important insight: among other things it makes realists construe (a) as saying that the independence of objects of knowledge from *acts of awareness* (*or thought, etc.*) *of them* entails the independence of objects of knowledge from thought or knowledge *tout court*. But there is of course no such entailment.

McDowell, it will be remembered, once said that if we accept an epistemically-constrained view of sense it would require us to adopt 'a novel, anti-realist conception of the world: if truth is not independent of our discovery of it, we must picture the world as our own creation or, at least, as springing up in response to our investigations. So verificationist objections to truth conditions conceptions of sense would have far-reaching metaphysical implications'.[7] This is an instructive remark, as immediately identifying rejection of the realist's independence claim with the thesis that the world is in some way causally dependent on the activity of making sense of thought and talk. This is not merely too quick: there is no connection between the two. It nicely illustrates the muddle we get into if we think it is metaphysics we are doing here.

In saying that realism is not a metaphysical but an epistemological thesis one is saying that it consists in a commitment to treating the mind-world relations as external or contingent ones. The opposing claim, that the relations are internal, is far from the claim that objects of thought are causally dependent upon thought (or more generally, experience or sentience) for their existence. Certain forms of idealism (for example, Berkeley's) put matters this way, and doubtless that is why some confuse idealism with anti-realism. Rather, it is at most the claim – until more is said – that no complete description of either relatum can leave out mention or the other.

It is important to see exactly what this means. In taking the view that the relation between thought and its objects (etc.) is contingent or external, the realist is saying that description of neither relatum essentially requires reference to the other. The

7 McDowell J., 'Truth-Values, Bivalence, and Verificationism' in *Truth and Meaning*, p. 48.

idiom of relations is very helpful here. A moment's reflection shows that the realist's externality claim is a mistake at least for the direction object-to-thought, for any account of the content of thoughts about things, and in particular the individuation of thoughts about things, essentially involves reference to the things thought about – this is the force of the least that can be said in favour of the notion of broad content. So realism offers us a peculiarly hybrid relation: external in the direction thought-to-things, internal in the direction things-to-thought. But it is an easy step for the anti-realist to show that thought about (perception of, theories of, etc.) things is always and inescapably present in, and therefore conditions, any full account of the things thought about; that is exactly the force of Putnam's arguments on this head; it is the nub of Berkeley's 'Master Argument';[8] and it rather well exemplified in the Copenhagen interpretation of quantum theory, in which descriptions of quantum phenomena are incomplete without reference to observers and conditions of observation. Such a view does not constitute a claim that the phenomena are caused by observations of them. No more does anti-realism claim this. However, a little thought shows that if this claim – that the relations between thought and things is internal – is correct, then one needs to think again about truth, objectivity, the modalities, and knowledge.

At this juncture one needs to stress again that because none of these points is metaphysical, anti-realism is not to be confused with idealism in any form. The former is, like the view it opposes, an epistemological thesis; the latter is a metaphysical one, or rather a family of such theses, having it that the universe is substantially mental. Its chief historical opposition is materialism, the thesis that the universe is made of matter – a view that should not, in turn, be confused with physicalism, which claims that the universe consists of what can be described by physics. What can be described by physics is not only not coterminous with matter, but might well entail that there is no such thing. (So Berkeley's 'immaterialism' is not idealism unless denial of the claim that the universe is material is conjoined with the positive claim that it is mental.) This point is overlooked if we thoughtlessly accept the

---

8 *Berkeley Principles*, sect. 23.

Cartesian dichotomy as exhausting the options. Berkeley implicitly recognised the problem: he argued, because he had to, for both a negative – immaterialist thesis – and a positive – idealist – thesis, because whereas the latter implies the former, the former does not imply the latter; it only makes room for it.[9]

So the point to iterate about realism is that what centrally defines it is the epistemological thesis that the domains or entities to which ontological commitment is made exist independently of knowledge of them. It is crucial to note that existential commitment without this epistemological independence claim is not realism. For no-one holds that some X is unreal if its existence can only be understood *via* what is involved in detecting X. Obviously, an anti-realist metaphysics is of course a metaphysics of existing things. What distinguishes such a view from a realist one is that unlike the realist, the anti-realist cannot understand metaphysical claims without a supporting epistemology that provides grounds for them. If something is asserted to exist, in other words, it is because something counts as supporting that claim; something counts as evidence for it, grasp of which plays its part in constituting the claim's sense. The anti-realist in this way regards the relations between existing things and the relevant kinds of epistemic access to them as internal ones – from which it does not follow, to repeat, that the existing things are causally or in any other metaphysical way dependent on cognition of them. This also is a hangover of misunderstandings of Berkeley, in which his denial of the existence of material substance is sometimes misread as denial of the existence of the physical world.

One can and therefore should object to the very label 'metaphysical realism'. What this phrase assumes or implies is that realism is a thesis about reality, that is, about what exists. But as we see, realists and their opponents do not disagree about what exists, but about how we are epistemically related to what exists. Part of the more general, and not exclusively philosophical, concern is of course to make sense of *another* kind of depend-

---

9 See Grayling, A. C., *Berkeley: The Central Arguments* (Duckworth, 1986) and 'Berkeley's Immaterialism' in Winkler (ed.) *Cambridge Companion to Berkeley* (CUP, 2002).

ence relation, namely, the way some things are said to exist dependently on other things (chairs on the elementary particles which constitute them, for example); but this too is ultimately a question of how we represent the world to ourselves (a question of our theories), and therefore is an epistemological question.

A corollary of this applies to Dummett's way with the question. He focused attention on truth as what, when understood in the realist's strong objectivist sense, gives his position content; and this led Dummett to treat the formal, value, and spatio-temporal cases together, as if 'truth' and 'realism' are to be understood univocally across them. In turn, that allows exportation from one formal case – the mathematical – of intuitionistic insights to the other cases. But it is a mistake to conflate the spatio-temporal case with the mathematical and value cases. For, whatever else 'realism' might denote, it at least denotes a thesis about a realm of entities. This, although a consequential insight, should not be a surprising one; even in traditional debates about universals and the spatio-temporal world this much is a common feature. But it allows that if ethics and mathematics are not about realms of entities, then controversies over the concepts of truth and knowledge applicable to them are not realism-anti-realism controversies. On this view, although one recognises that, in ethics, the parties to the debate are cognitivists and those who disagree with them, and that in mathematics the parties are espousers of different conceptions of what makes for the truth of mathematical statements, we also recognise that in neither debate is it just that there is no obligation to talk about the existence of entities (the respective candidates might be 'moral properties', and 'structures' – say, sets); it is, as Dummett himself suggests, positively misleading. For if, respectively, cognitivist and Platonist theses turn on claims about the existence of certain sorts of moral properties or mathematical structures, the question immediately arises as to how we can reduce the metaphorical character of such claims, given that their sense is imported from the one case (the spatio-temporal case) which alone has unmetaphorical content. The absence of an answer to this question is precisely Dummett's motive for switching attention from the problem of existence to the problem of truth. But doing so brings too much under one label. The solution is not to find a different reason – one given in terms of truth – for classifying these controversies together, but instead to recognise that they are controversies of quite different kinds. So we do well to restrict talk of realism to the case where controversy concerns unmetaphorical claims about the knowledge-independent existence of entities or realms of entities – namely, the spatio-temporal case – and to employ more precise denominations for the different debates which arise in other, different, domains.

If metaphysics is altogether not to the point – if our metaphysics is always our choice of model for the most effective means of anticipating experience, and as revisable when pragmatic considerations require – then representation is certainly metaphysically innocent. But our ways of representing the world are not innocent: a non-arbitrary, experience-constrained picture of the world has massive practical consequences (at the outer limit, it affects our chances of survival as individuals and as a species), and its structure determines the inferences we can draw from any current evidence in the presence of those large commitments of our conceptual scheme which serve as its general premises. So representation is never epistemically innocent: and that is an insight which in my view makes a big difference to how we proceed in most of the rest of philosophy. It tells us much about the right way to view rationality, truth, meaning, and the nature and mutual relationships of our most revision-resistant beliefs: all of which makes for another long and interesting tale.

But one important concluding observation can be made, in clarification of the *nature* of the debate in which realists, anti-realists and those like Putnam who pronounce a plague on both their houses, are engaged. This is to recognise that the debate is entirely a second-order one, in the following sense. Ordinary discourse is, without question, realist in character. We assume that the entities we refer to exist independently of our cognising them, and we assume the same about the states of affairs which, we further assume, make true or false our assertions about them.

This realism at the level of ordinary discourse, the first order level, is rather promiscuous: we take literally a sense, to be informatively compared with the case of fictional discourse, of there being something we are talking about when we talk. Various ways of cashing this thought suggest themselves, one of which is

that it would render explanation of our first order linguistic practices incoherent if we did not or could not attribute to speakers
beliefs about the existence, independently of them, of the entities
constituting the domain over which their discourse ranges. Nor
would we have any purchase on the family of concepts collected
under the heading 'representation' without at least the heuristic
of the mind-world divide that these realist commitments involve.

But these realist commitments are *commitments* and there is
no automatic entailment from the fact that they are fundamental
to first order practice to their being literally true. We can now
distinguish between the realistic assumptions of the first order,
and the second order thesis that realism is literally true. Call this
'metarealism'. On this way of putting matters, anti-realism
should more correctly be described as anti-metarealism, and
consists, on the most precise reading, in the thesis that it is
mistaken to claim that realism is literally true, for the now familiar reasons. The dispute between these two positions is accordingly a second order controversy about the correct understanding
of our first order practice and its presuppositions. Second order
commentary might show that there is need to revise a first order
practice wherever the commentary reveals the practice to be
wrong. A second order thesis like this would constitute an error
theory with respect to first order practice. But it depends on cases
and on argument, for it can be that second order interpretation of
first order practice leaves the latter as it is.

At first sight the difference between the metarealist and anti-
metarealist position looks vanishingly small. The former says that
the first order realist commitments are literally true, the latter
that they are assumptions, perhaps undischargeable ones as
transcendental arguments might show. But the consequences for
a range of issues, including our understanding of truth and
knowledge, are great. On the metarealist view the relations
between speakers and what they speak about are as we have
seen external ones, so it is at very least natural to treat truth as a
property conferred on our utterances by knowledge-independent
circumstances, and our notion of knowledge, in turn, as having it
that whatever consequences, if any, our knowing something
about the world has for the world, they are contingent ones only.
In particular, coming to know things about the world is a process

of discovery, one which lies under the austere constraint of our inherent epistemic limitations. Taken together, these theses about truth and knowledge entail commitment to there being a sharp distinction between truth-value and grounds for assigning truth-value – just the epistemological commitment, as we saw, identified by both Dummett and Putnam as fundamental to realism in the sense of metarealism. For the anti-metarealists, that distinction exists for us only at the first order level, as a matter of epistemic strategy.

Either way, therefore, the nub of the matter at the second order concerns the question whether the metaphysical commitments at the first order can be regarded as literally true (or false), or as having an irreducibly strategic character, constituting assumptions of our discourse which we hold true as a framework for anticipating experience fruitfully. It is a debate primarily about the role of epistemic constraints in understanding our thought, not a debate about what logical principles our practices should embody, nor a debate about what is taken to exist on our first order scheme of things (or the science by which they are explained and, to the extent possible, manipulated). In this sense the debate leaves everything as it is, and therefore if anti-metarealism is correct, no revisions to logic, linguistic practice or mundane metaphysics are called for. Note especially its conservatism with respect to classical logic and the ontology of folk physics. And it leaves in place, at the first order, all our standard practices and assumptions about representation. This marks a sharp contrast with revisionary versions of anti-realism, as espoused for example by Dummett and Tennant, as well as *outré* post-modern relativistic versions of anti-realism like Rorty's. And it arrives at a terminus not too distant from, but better motivated than, Putnam's view that the mind-world relations, though internal – that is, though not epistemically innocent – are metaphysically so.

3

Truth and evaluation

Theories of truth may be said to fall into two classes. One consists in those theories stating that truth is a *substantive property* of whatever the truth-bearers are. The property might be a relational one, where the relation is (familiarly) some form of correspondence or coherence; or a functional one, for example epistemic utility, as in the pragmatic theory. A further member of this class asserts that truth is a substantial but *indefinable* property; Donald Davidson takes such a view.[1]

The other class comprises theories stating that truth is not a substantive notion; *there is nothing more to truth*, these theories say, than use of the predicate '... is true' as a convenience for certain logical and rhetorical purposes. Such views are called, for obvious reasons, 'deflationary' theories.

The merits of these various views about truth have been, and continue to be, much debated. I shall not add to that debate here, but offer instead a sketch of an argument – better: a sketch of how an argument might look in outline – to suggest that truth is neither deflatable nor indefinable, but consists in a family of cognitively significant notions. Among its side benefits this suggestion offers us a diagnosis of why traditional theories of truth are unsatisfactory – but it also hints at what is right about them. It suggests further that Ramsey is right about truth in a certain respect; namely, that the important task is to state a theory of assertion. But successor conceptions of his redundancy account get no comfort here, for the suggestion is that truth is not one insubstantial thing, but many substantial things, none of which is truth as attempts have traditionally been made to define it.

---

1 See Davidson in any of 'Reality without Reference', 'A Coherence Theory of Truth and Knowledge', 'The Content of Truth', 'The Folly of Trying to Define Truth', *op. cit.*

First one needs to recall something about the way certain expressions function. Consider the words *thing, do, nice*. 'Thing' does general duty for any noun, 'do' for any or at least many active verbs, 'nice' for any adjective of a generally positive purport. It might be illuminating to call each respectively a 'substitute' or 'dummy' noun/verb/adjective, because each marks places in sentences where more precise expressions go when the utterer is less hurried or lazy. In fact, with a nod towards 'pronouns of laziness' (because although they are not essentially anaphoric, they can have such uses) one might describe these expressions as 'lazy' to give an informative contrast with 'busy expressions' that do more precise and particular work.

For the purpose in hand I introduce a notion of 'lazy predicates', to be understood as expressions marking a place in sentences for more precise property-denoting expressions. As with the lazy expressions just cited, the lazy predicate tells us something about the range and kind of the busier substitutes it takes: its use implies that whatever the busier predicates are, employment of them implies observance of certain constraints, or at least the aspiration to achieve certain desiderata. So the lazy expressions are not mere dummies. There are in fact quite a number of lazy predicates, and they play important roles in the economy of thought. Something more is said about this later. At this point the task is to use the notion of a lazy predicate to sketch the present suggestion about truth, as follows.

The predicate '_is true' is a lazy predicate. It holds a place for more precise predicates, denoting evaluatory properties appropriate to the discourse in which possession of those properties is valued. The properties are explicitly discourse-sensitive properties. As examples one might cite candidates from the history of related debates: verification in the case of discourse about the spatio-temporal realm; constructability in the case of a certain view about mathematics; (say) universalisability in the case of ethical claims. These are merely examples of more specific properties; well-known debates about these candidates do not make one confident that they are the right ones; and to add to dissatisfaction with at least some of them one might suggest that, anyway, different subdiscourses are themselves likely to vary the evaluations (and associated evaluatory procedures) for which saying '_is true' goes proxy. To see the point one need only think of the difference between talk of Quakers and talk of quarks, both in some sense referents in what we take to be an explanatorily-continuous domain. Indeed the situation is even more complex: how we evaluate perceptual claims, tensed claims, theoretical claims, claims about social objects (and much besides) is a highly various matter; yet in some sense such claims relate to a unified world of temporal and spatio-temporal things, so this is independent of the differences between such evaluations and those applicable to purely formal realms and – differently again – different value realms.

A proponent of this suggestion need not argue for any specific set of values and evaluatory procedures for given discourses at this stage, since to do so is to engage in the appropriate philosophical enquiry itself. The concern at this stage is more general: it is to find and state general constraints on evaluations which reveal why the same lazy predicate '_is true' collects them all.

Evaluation is an epistemic matter in many cases, but not in all. The aesthetic case and aspects of the moral case are not so – and this observation is important, for the reason that since evaluation is about identifying and measuring value, it might be natural to think that there are fruitful comparisons to be drawn between busy substituends of '_is true' on the one hand, and '_is good' and '_is beautiful' on the other. But the comparisons are not smooth, and this suggests that general constraints on evaluation will have to be understood disjunctively – some evaluations are constrained by one subset of constraints, others by others, and as usual one major interest lies in seeing whether the subsets share any common members.

To summarise matters so far: the suggestion is that a theory of truth is (a) globally, a theory of evaluation, and (b) locally, a theory of subject-matter-specific evaluations for different given discourses. More circumstantially, the idea is that the busy substituends of '_is true' are predicates that denote evaluatory properties of such kinds as, or in appropriate cases better specified than, *verification, constructability, universalisabilty* (and so on for discourses not mentioned). As just noted: the task is not one of making out some particular local theory of evaluation, but to say something general about evaluation.

We wish to evaluate propositions, claims, beliefs, theories. I shall speak generally of evaluating propositions. What is it to evaluate – to assess the value of – something? Consider a sheep-dog. We know what we need it for, and what we need it to be like; and if it answers our needs, and performs as required, we value it – and if it does not, we disvalue it. We need it to herd sheep, not eat them or frighten them; so we require that it be docile and responsive to command, and to have the appropriate temperament. These are among the desiderata it has to satisfy, which can be summarised by saying that *it has to be apt for the job we wish it to do*. As regards propositions, we naturally wish them to be true, because then we can rely on them in inference, we can trust them to convey information about how things are, we can use them to test other claims, we can agree on them (at least eventually, as providing the stable points on which we can converge); and because they exercise rational authority over us and therefore provide tests for norms of rationality. Moreover, we are entitled to assert them, and they are typically more useful than false ones.

Compare this list of desiderata for truth with what we wish to say about evaluation. If, on the basis of evaluatory procedures appropriate to their domain, we are to attach 'value' (antonym: disvalue) to claims, what we mean is that we at least require them to be:

(1) reliable in inference;
(2) consistent with other propositions we value;
(3) usable in evaluating other propositions;
(4) agreement-inviting/promoting;
(5) authoritative for us in the domain;
(6) such as to entitle us to assert them;
(7) such that acceptance of them is a norm for rationality;
(8) such that they help us organise the subject-matter they concern more effectively – by appropriate and negotiated standards of effectiveness – than competitors.

This list has some overlaps with the list for truth, but is more inclusive. Neither list is non-redundant. Some items in both are restatements of one or more others. I list them in this way to bring out aspects of the desiderata. In both it may be that what occurs as (6) in the evaluation list – *viz.* assertibility – is something which the others constitute, as the principal mark and chief point of value – including the case where value is taken to be unanalysed truth.

A valued proposition, by satisfying these desiderata, accordingly has these properties:

A. Acceptability: it invites acceptance on grounds that involve negotiated ways of maximising agreement on a triangulation of evidence, aims and context. This is not just (4); it is all of (1)–(7) in the list of desiderata.

B. Adequacy: that is, fittingness or appropriateness for the task of meeting needs in that domain of concerns; (1), (5).

C. Utility: it does the job of providing information, generating predictions, licensing inferences, settling disputes; (1), (3), (5).

D. Stability: it forms part of a view (for the domain) which is cogent, stable, robust in tests and other demands upon it; (2), (6), (7); it is thus a 'fact' for the domain; (1), (5), (6).

Disvalued propositions are those that fail to have at least A and C because they fail to satisfy the desiderata (but note that (4) and (8) can – for a time – be failed by, for example, novel ideas). Disvalued propositions are rejected. In ordinary parlance we call them 'false' but even when we are using our lazy predicate 'true' it would be more correct to call them 'not true' to mark the fact that there are different ways in which they can fail to be true other than by being false (for example: by being meaningless, inappropriate to the domain, neither true nor false, and so forth).

We allow ourselves to talk of information being conveyed by true propositions. This is allied to the notion of fact, which is what true propositions are said to correspond to. The chief use of this is in inference: having information enables one to get to further information. (It might also just be satisfying to know it.) On the evaluation theory there is no mention of information or facts; nevertheless we can say, regarding desiderata (1), (5), (6) that a valued proposition is a fact in the sense that it has the property of standing firm for the domain.

If you take a subdomain of the spatio-temporal case, or a formal case, or an ethical or aesthetic case, the content of evaluations and the procedures involved in them will be specific to the subject-matter in hand. We can evaluate sheep-dogs and we can evaluate grand pianos, but although we can say general things about what we are looking for (not (1)–(8) for here we are evaluating things, not claims or theories), the specifics will differ. If we thought that there must be one thing that all evaluation consists in or results in, then we would find ourselves testing, say, to see whether Steinways bite sheep. Although it is surely true of Steinways that they do not bite sheep, this cannot be what we want them for. Saying this is what is meant by denying that truth is a univocal concept.

To say that '_is true' is a dummy for '_is constructible', '_is verifiable', and so for other cases, is to say that there are, literally, different kinds of truth, individuated by subject-matter. Tarski suspected that this might be so.[2] And in line with his hint, this theory is consistent with the view that 'truth' in formal languages should anyway be considered quite separately; the idea being that talk of the *semantics* of a formal language is actually metaphorical, so that what is called 'truth' (or 'constructability', say) is in fact a metalinguistic description of a syntactic property, such (on some, if controversial, views) being the only kind of properties formal languages have.

But to say that there are literally different kinds of truth is not to make a relativist remark: the discussion here has nothing to do with such claims as that different points of view upon the same subject-matter can legitimately result in different distributions of truth-value across the propositions expressing it. That suspect claim is the subject of a different debate.

So much is the merest sketch of a theory, but it offers resistance to the deflationary thought that it is a misconception to think that there is a property denoted by 'truth' with explanatory structure. This theory says that there are a number of such properties, which allow 'is true' to serve lazily for them all because the global desiderata apply to them all in virtue of their epistemic role. This

---

2 Tarski, A., 'The Concept of Truth in Formalised Languages', in (trans. Woodger J. H.), *Logic, Semantics, Metamathematics* (Oxford, 1956), pp. 152–278; and (a very good introduction) Tarski, A., 'The Semantic Conception of Truth', in Feigl, H., and Sellars, W., *Readings in Philosophical Analysis* (New York, 1949), pp. 52–84.

sketch therefore offers a theory which says that truth is not one thing, still less one miminal thing, but lots of substantial things. If it is agnate to any theories in the tradition of debate on the subject, its closest relative might be a version of a pragmatic theory.[3]

---

3 The argument here has its original in a section of chapter 6 of my *Philosophical Logic* (3rd ed., 1997). I am grateful to those who encouraged me to give it an independent statement; and to Alex Orenstein for discussion of 'dummy/lazy predicates'.

4

Truth and indefinability

The idea that truth is a substantial but indefinable property is a seductive one, for if it is right the task of investigating meaning, knowledge, validity, and other central philosophical concerns turns out to be much easier than we thought. Donald Davidson offers an influential version of this idea. What follows is an examination of his view. I have no quarrel with that aspect of his view which treats truth as an explanatorily rich property of whatever the truth-bearers are, so my criticisms are not motivated by minimalism about truth. Instead, my focus is his indefinability claim, which is crucial because it is what makes Davidson's notion of truth costlessly available for the purposes described.

'Truth is beautifully transparent compared to belief and coherence,' Davidson claims, 'and I shall take it as primitive.'[1] The comparison is drawn because whereas belief and coherence might be thought necessary for a definition of truth as coherence among beliefs, Davidson has no intention of so defining it. There is a strong connection being made here between the conceptions of primitiveness and indefinability: Davidson assumes that if truth is primitive it is indefinable. This strategy – of identifying, or perhaps nominating, a given concept as primitive and therefore as indefinable – turns out to recommend itself generally to Davidson as a way of dealing with most major concepts in philosophy.

In the introduction to his paper 'The Folly of Trying to Define Truth'[2] Davidson tells us how to approach questions about the concept of truth and by extension other major concepts, includ-

---

1 Donald Davidson 'The Coherence Theory of Truth and Knowledge' in LePore E. (ed.), *Truth and Interpretation* (Oxford: Blackwell, 1986), p. 308.
2 Donald Davidson, 'The Folly of Trying to Define Truth' in *The Journal of Philosophy*, Vol. XCIII (June 1996), pp. 263–278.

ing belief, memory, perception and causality. His prescription is that instead of seeking definitions of these concepts we should settle for tracing connections among them, for whereas the attempt to define them is bound to fail, exhibiting their interrelations is clarifying and informative. (Although Davidson does not cite Strawson, the idea of 'tracing connections' is precisely how Strawson defines the aim of 'descriptive metaphysics' in *Individuals*; so Davidson's proposal has a good pedigree.)

Davidson supports his case against definition by offering a cautionary tale, concerning the failure of Socrates ever to arrive at what he seeks in Plato's earlier dialogues, namely, definitions of beauty, courage, justice and other important notions. Socrates' quest is bound to fail, says Davidson, because he seeks a *sharp* answer to the questions (where X is holiness or beauty or some such) 'what is Xness?', 'what makes X things X?'. And Socrates does not accept definition by extensional paradigms, that is, proffered examples of, say, beautiful people or just actions; he is interested only in essences.

Davidson describes the kind of definition Socrates mistakenly seeks as *reduction* of a target concept to 'other concepts that are simpler, clearer and more basic'.[3] He alternatively describes this style of definition as the 'formulation in a clearer, more basic vocabulary' of the elements that must figure in the analysis of some concept.[4] His chief point is that Plato failed to notice that some philosophically important concepts are not amenable to such definition. When you add the fact that in discussing one concept – say, knowledge – philosophers typically pretend they understand the other concepts required – in this case, at least truth and belief – you see a moral: in Davidson's words: 'however feeble or faulty our attempts to relate these various basic concepts to each other, these attempts fare better, and teach us more, than our efforts to produce correct and revealing definitions of basic concepts in terms of clearer or more fundamental concepts.'[5]

---

3 *Ibid.*, p. 263.
4 *Ibid.*
5 *Ibid.*, p. 264.

Davidson remarks that this is only to be expected, because the concepts that attract philosophical attention – he lists *truth*, *action*, *knowledge*, *belief*, *cause*, the *good* and the *right* – are 'the most elementary concepts we have' without which we might not have any others. So why do we presume that they can be definitionally reduced to simpler, more basic concepts? 'We should', he concludes, 'accept the fact that what makes these concepts so important must also foreclose on the possibility of finding a foundation for them which reaches deeper into bedrock.'[6]

And this insight is to be applied to the concept of truth: we cannot hope 'to underpin it with something more transparent or easier to grasp'; it is indefinable.[7] Nevertheless: to say that truth – along with the important concepts – is indefinable is not to say that nothing revealing can be said about it, or that it is 'mysterious, ambiguous, or untrustworthy', for the strategy of tracing its connections with other concepts (such as belief, desire and action) shows otherwise.[8]

Such, in essence, is Davidson's view. There is much to say about each of its component aspects.

Davidson's claim that most philosophically significant concepts are the most elementary and basic concepts we have invites comment.[9] There would be near consensus that the concepts he lists are indeed among the most important. The quite different claim that they are the most *elementary* and the most *basic* are a different matter. Consider first the latter claim. To say that these concepts are the most basic – even in the weaker sense that they are the most basic in some respect or for some discourse – precisely constitutes the substance of much philosophical debate, against which it begs the question simply to assert that they are. Every one of the listed concepts has, familiarly, been subjected to detailed attempts at analysis – the standard endeavours are scarcely in need of rehearsal: 'knowledge' into justified true belief, 'truth' into correspondence or coherence relations, 'causation' into temporally sequential necessary conjunctions of

---

6 *Ibid.*, pp. 264–265.
7 *Ibid.*
8 *Ibid.*
9 *Ibid.*

events, and so on. It is Davidson's claim that these efforts are misconceived. Traditional approaches have taken it, on the contrary, that the reason for interest in 'know', 'cause' and the rest is that perplexities attend many uses of them and that these perplexities demonstrate that we are insufficiently clear about what we mean by them. On Davidson's view, sufficient clarity can be generated by seeing how 'true', 'believes' and the others connect, without attempting to understand 'truth', 'belief' and the others *as such*.

Now, it might be the result of a Strawsonian enquiry – it is certainly the aim of Strawson's own version of such enquiry – into the order of dependence among our concepts in general that we can specify which are more and which are less basic, but to begin such an enquiry with an ordering assumed renders such enquiry pointless. Such would be the result of *specifying* that 'truth', 'belief' and the others are 'basic' concepts. But this thought, in turn, suggests a respect in which a Strawsonian strategy – and as it happens, Strawson's own strategy – seems not to fit Davidson's bill in any case. As noted, for Strawson a major part of the tracing task is to identify the order of dependence among concepts, with the target, or at least the guiding ideal, being the discovery of which occupants of the logical space under scrutiny are fundamental to others. This strategy naturally fits one that finds transcendental arguments a useful device for identifying fundamental concepts, for their purpose is to show which concepts must be in one's possession as a condition for the possession of given others. This strategy, when successful, offers an anchorage in certain concepts which, although they might not turn out to be simpler than the concepts whose possession they make possible (for example: the concept of a physical object is more basic but more complex than the concept of an ice-cream), would by the argument be more fundamental, and might therefore constitute a resource for analysis or even definition of non-fundamental concepts. It seems implicit in the Strawsonian strategy, in other words, that tracing connections yields an ordering of the more and the less fundamental; and analysis is thereby made possible.

The question whether a concept is basic is quite different again from the question whether it is elementary or simple (as the ice-cream example just used shows). Basic concepts can be complex, and arguably many are. That is why we think them in need of analysis, or explication, or perhaps even definition. Elementary or simple concepts are those which are by definition *incapable of further analysis*. But this by itself – and this point arises again below – does not mean that they are *incapable of definition*. It again begs questions to label a concept elementary if the point is thereby to warrant its indefinability, for these are not the same thing.

To call a concept 'elementary' is to accord it a distinctive structural role in some conceptual edifice – in effect, a foundational one. When the foundation in question is that of our thought we require the elements to be more exact and perspicuous than less elementary parts of the structure – that is, than the dependent concepts in the scheme. But this is obviously, in fact notoriously, not so with the concepts Davidson describes as elementary.

An aside is invited by Davidson's remark that 'we should accept the fact that what makes these concepts so important must also foreclose on the possibility of finding a foundation for them which reaches deeper into bedrock'. It is that one has to guard against versions of what might be called the 'argument from impotence', employed (for a notable example) by Descartes in saying that the mind-body problem is best solved by being ignored because it defeats human understanding, a view shared by those (such as McGinn) who claim that humans are constitutionally barred from knowing how consciousness arises from brain-function. Such arguments are an objectionable resource in philosophy if their effect is to release one from the obligation to think about the hard problems, which is the opposite of what one should be doing. For present purposes, the remark suggests that Davidson's version of the Strawsonian strategy sees it as tracing conceptual connections on the same epistemic and logical level; it is an anti-foundational version of the strategy; and this arguably compounds what is anyway the most serious limitation of the strategy: its invitation to a form of relativism not catered for by Davidson's other well-known anti-relativistic arguments.[10]

---

10 See Davidson, D., 'On the Very Idea of a Conceptual Scheme' in *Inquiries into Truth and Interpretation* (Oxford: Oxford University Press, 1984), and 'The Myth of the Subjective' in Kraus, M. (ed.), *Relativism: Interpretation and Confrontation* (Notre Dame, 1989), chap. 9.

The worst problem with allegedly elementary concepts, as with allegedly indefinable ones, is that they can be over-permissive. Specifying a concept as elementary or indefinable, without also specifying constraints on its use, carries a risk. It is that such concepts permit too much in the way of inference. Consider this comparison: suppose you count into your scheme the concept of an omnipotent deity. Then almost anything goes: because, for example, the laws of nature can be suspended at any time, in any way, and therefore practically nothing is ruled out as to what can and might happen. The rider 'almost anything goes' is added because one does not know whether an omnipotent deity can do logically impossible things, or eat himself for breakfast, and so forth. But almost everything else goes. So we approximate to the acceptance of a contradiction as a premise: here absolutely anything goes. Simple or indefinable concepts, if unconstrained, or not subjected to the government of conditions of application, are over-permissive in this way, allowing anything or at least too much to be thought or inferred. But the danger is that if anything or too much is licensed by employment of some concept, nothing or too little of any use is. This is a cousin of the thought that if a theory explains everything and accommodates all cases, it explains nothing.

To deal with this problem Davidson says that although truth is indefinable, this does not mean that there is nothing revealing to be said about truth. Since the revelations arise in tracing conceptual connections, it is crucial to examine the 'connection tracing' strategy more closely.

Consider the sentence, 'He has Jupiter on the midheaven, with Sagittarius rising, and Mars in the seventh house'. This introduces a spate of concepts whose interrelations, once grasped, clarify one another. But the question is not whether astrological concepts clarify one another by their interrelations, but whether any sort of reality answers to them; or more weakly, whether they stand up to careful scrutiny, however well they hang together from an internal perspective – for 'hanging together well' is by itself insufficient to legitimate them.

Davidson might say that this misses a point, namely, that these clusters of concepts must themselves relate to yet others in the larger discourse, and our adjudications of their value flow from understanding those larger relations. For a different example: theological claims compete for the truth with scientific ones over such matters as the origin of the universe, or whether water can turn into wine without the help of grapes; and when we see how the concepts domiciled in each more largely relate to others, we see which are the more acceptable.

But this reply only enlarges the scope of the difficulty. Contrast the Strawsonian strategy with what looks like a legitimate ambition to understand individual concepts (no insignificant matter even for the task of ascertaining how the nature of each influences the relations it can have with others) and to find some maximally stable basis for doing so in the light of how things are in the world, or in the limits of experience, or in the constraints of logic or at least of rationality – all in the hope of securing objectivity, or its closest approximation, for them. This is not something a Strawsonian strategy even tries to offer. The Strawsonian strategy offers an account only of *relations among concepts*; and therefore what applies to theological or astrological concepts as a family – namely, that the Strawsonian strategy offers no guide to their legitimacy or justification beyond what that family of concepts internally claims for itself – applies to the whole family of all our concepts. The problem can be shortly stated by saying that we do not escape what is wrong with parochiality and relativism by claiming that the whole scheme is the parish. (Rorty finds Davidson's views agreeable for this very reason: which suggests some familiar forms of criticism.) It therefore has to be questioned how far anything has even been clarified (still less justified, though Davidson repudiates this as an aim) if the terminus of enquiry is just: an internal mapping of connections.

What is at stake here is the question of *objectivity*, and the problem is that the Strawson-like strategy of tracing conceptual connections appears not to provide it. A feature of Davidson's views – his 'externalism' – might be supposed to help here.

Davidson holds that language-users understand one another by being interpreters of one other's utterances. Interpretation at its simplest is a mutual activity of two speakers who share experience of a portion of the world, and who hold each other's beliefs about that portion of the world to be true (the interpretative principle that another's beliefs are largely true is the 'Principle of

Charity'). The two speakers, and the portion of the world available to both, form a triangle. The three-way relation underwriting mutual interpretation is called 'triangulation'. It is this that might secure the objectivity that the Strawsonian strategy fails to provide.

We learn from Davidson's views about triangulation that this essentially relational condition of interpretation is tied to the causal role of the world in giving beliefs their content. Events in the world cause beliefs, Davidson says, in a 'fairly direct' way by sensory stimulation; we have to connect beliefs with what they are about as regards their empirical content – truth-value and empirical content come from perception, or more precisely, the circumstances of perception.

So far, these remarks have a reassuringly familiar ring. But their tendency is not, it turns out, to give our beliefs extra-mental anchorage of the kind offered in traditional theories. Davidson's talk of the 'environment, the shared distal stimulation' that plays a part in causing our beliefs is, first, not talk of what provides justification for them. Only beliefs can be evidence for beliefs; what gives rise to beliefs cannot. A dualism between our concepts and what they are of – their content – is rejected because there cannot be content by itself, and because it is not propositionally articulated, and therefore cannot do what empiricists want it to do, namely, provide warrant for the scheme.[11] This rejects the empiricist claim that sensory awareness is the uniquely authoritative source of contingent knowledge.

Nor is the relation between the apex of the triangle in triangulation and its base angles to be understood as connected to a familiar set of variously related other relations: perception and its objects, thought about things, truth and its makers, reference and singled-out bits of the world. Davidson rejects all these, or at least – in the case of reference – accepts only a severely deflated version, as conceptually toxic versions or by-products of the scheme-content dualism.[12]

---

11 Davidson, D., 'On the very Idea of a Conceptual Scheme', *op. cit.*

12 See Davidson, D., in any of 'Reality without Reference', 'A Coherence Theory of Truth and Knowledge', 'The Content of Truth', 'The Folly of Trying to Define Truth', *op. cit.*

So we know what is *not* meant by talk of 'the world' in Davidson, and we note that it consorts well with a particular choice of emphasis. The objectivity of our concepts on what Davidson calls 'the social or externalist view' is a function of the mutuality of interpretation. In setting out this view Davidson gives the environment an error-or-divergence-adjusting role, but 'nature does not speak to us', it is not on its own a contributor to meaning. For meaning we must look to mutual interpretation, and interpretation is *essentially* social. Objectivity for Davidson is therefore intersubjectivity. And this is consistent both with the coherence flavour of much that Davidson says – 'no point in looking outside sentences' as he puts it – and his advocacy of a Strawsonian strategy.

Despite having entitled a paper 'A Coherence Theory of Truth and Knowledge', Davidson dislikes the coherence label, and for the very reason identified above as a flaw in the Strawsonian strategy, namely, that it provides only internal justification for beliefs. The point can be put by saying that in addition to seeing connections between beliefs, we need a reason to think that most of them are true. And familiarly, instead of seeking an external anchorage to provide this assurance, Davidson thinks that we have one in the Principle of Charity. To get our interpretations of others going, we must take it that most of their beliefs are true. So let us just do ourselves the same good turn, and take it that most of the beliefs in our own scheme are true. The principle is: 'belief is in its nature veridical'. Here then is a further feature of the interpretational considerations that yield objectivity.[13]

Two large objections suggest themselves. First, one is left feeling multiply dissatisfied with the claim that one can invoke 'the world' as playing a causal role in determining the content of beliefs, and that one can invoke 'bits of the world' to serve in a lean account of reference, while at the same time being told that these relations have nothing to do with questions of meaning and epistemic justification.

Dissatisfaction is prompted when a notion of 'the distal', or 'the environment of communication', or just 'the world', is

---

13 'A Coherence Theory of Truth and Knowledge', *op. cit.*, p. 309.

invoked to tidy the edges of a theory which has no substantive role for them, when one wants to know – in relation to 'the world' or 'the environment of communication' – something about how the concepts of knowledge, truth and meaning engage with our interest in 'the world', by no means an intuitively misplaced concern. After all, we take language to range over an independently existing realm of spatio-temporal items, including events, and we wish to know – that is, to have a way of recognising – which sentences about this realm are true, so that we can know what we can know: for we have severely practical interests at stake in the world.

The dissatisfaction here is with Davidson's seeming to have and eat several cakes at once. It is prompted, for example, by the opening paragraphs of 'A Coherence Theory of Truth and Knowledge', where Davidson speaks of 'meaning being given by *objective truth conditions*' which can be satisfied (that is, by a thought-independent world), while yet *it is absurd to speak of a confrontation between belief and reality*. We can be *realists* and 'can *insist that knowledge is of an objective world independent of our thought and language*', but no sense attaches to talking about a '*scheme-content duality*' (a duality between thought and language, on the one hand, and an objective world on the other).[14]

Secondly, Davidson's way out of the coherence problem prompts questions. It rests on the claim that 'coherent belief is in its nature veridical'.[15] But the history of science suggests that this claim is false, and that beyond its being an hypothesis with some utility in getting radical interpretation *started*, it is not an invariably good guide otherwise. For in understanding others, one often has to understand that what they are saying is false, or at least, that they hold certain beliefs true which we take to be false, perhaps for the reason that they are in error, or lying. These two points need to be taken together. The history of science teaches that the truth and the utility – within limits – of our beliefs do not invariably coincide, and historically have been systematically divergent; and the point about falsehoods suggests that the false

---

14 *Ibid.*, p. 307.
15 *Ibid.*, p. 309.

beliefs, ignorance, interests, or even malice of others can undermine our confidence in their reliability as truth-tellers, so that the interpretation of their discourse must surely make plenty of room for defeasibility. Taken together, we find that the principle of charity is questionable beyond its heuristic applications.

These dissatisfactions over objectivity prompt questions. Davidson (a) urges the Strawsonian strategy, and commits himself to what we might for convenience call the coherence plus charity view (coherentism saved by the principle of the inherent veridicality of belief). He also says (b) that the world plays a part in causing our beliefs. But then he also says (c) that the world's causal activity with respect to us does not enter into the justification of our beliefs, and is not therefore the source of their objectivity – which, instead, is social. (d) Meanings – reverting to the coherence mode – are functions of mutual interpretation. But (e) the world contributes to the empirical content of our beliefs, and (f) perceptual beliefs are basic to empirical knowledge.

Views (a), (c) and (d) do not seem to be consistent with (b), (e) and (f). If they are consistent, they have to be made so on the grounds of the fine detail of their supporting argument – and by appropriate analysis or definition of the concepts which crucially figure in them: 'belief', 'veridicality', 'coherence', 'cause', 'justification', 'social', 'meaning', 'interpretation', 'empirical content', 'perception', and 'knowledge'. It will scarcely do to claim that these are all elementary, basic, primitive and indefinable. If it is not folly to try to understand these concepts better, neither can it be so to understand the concept deeply implicated in most of them, *viz.* truth.

We reach this point as a result of canvassing Davidson's alternative to the 'Socratic' method of defining concepts. Central to Davidson's claim that it is folly to 'define' truth is therefore what he means by 'definition'. And what he means by 'definition' turns out on examination to be surprisingly partial and inadequate. There are senses of 'definition', and more to the point of 'analysis', which Davidson ignores or appears to confuse with one another, and which arguably provide far stronger alternatives to – or in some cases adjuncts to – the Strawsonian strategy.[16]

---

16 It is important to note something about the historical prefigurings Davidson appeals to in describing his preferred strategy, *viz.* that of tracing connections

One might begin by remarking, in connection with Davidson's strictures upon Socrates, that the latter's refusal to accept definition by extensional paradigms is a mistake. This form of definition operates by giving focal examples, grasping which as such enables normally intelligent persons to apply the concept thereafter in usual conformity with fellow-conceptualisers. Many general concepts, such as those of colours, are not amenable to definition by the statement of necessary and sufficient conditions for their application; rather, they are learned and used on the basis of agreements about focal cases, focal non-cases, and shared hesitancies at the margins. The ability to display the right skills in application, and to behave in closely similar ways to other conceptualisers in cases of vagueness, constitutes our test of whether someone has mastery of given concepts. *Mutatis mutandis*, the same applies for mastery of the general terms that denote them.

This prompts one to remember that there are many kinds of definition. This is not the place for a detailed taxonomy, but it is

---

among concepts. Davidson contrasts this tracing strategy with the alternative of trying to arrive at definitions – by which, as the main text notes, he means: trying to understand what is problematic in terms of something clearer, simpler, or more fundamental. He calls – I should say miscalls – this latter strategy 'Socratic'. It is a case of miscalling because if it is to have a useful name it should rather be described as Russellian. This is because Davidson has chosen to view definition as if it were in effect analysis, which Russell distinguishes sharply from definition. Socratic definition, so far as it can be separated from Platonic definition associated with the theory of Forms, is *specification of the essence* of whatever is at issue – typically, an abstract reality such as Piety or Goodness. (Plato took it that his theory of Forms offers an account of this which is lacking in Socrates, although his procedure can also sometimes be construed as definition of concepts rather than things, however conceived, as when in the *Theaetetus* he discusses knowledge.) Now the point of remarking these historical prefigurings is that they help to clarify Davidson's argument. He identifies definition with the Russell-like strategy of analysing concepts into their clearer and simpler elements, cites examples of how this fails, and urges in its place a Strawson-like strategy of tracing conceptual connections. I give reason for saying that the two strategies are not exclusive; that the Russellian strategy has much going for it, but is not one of stating definitions (Russell, to repeat, expressly conceived analysis as being distinct from definition); that the Strawsonian strategy is not entirely satisfactory for Davidson's purposes – and that anyway (as I shortly show) that it suffers a severe limitation.

helpful to recall the following, doubtless incomplete, assortment. There is 'analytic definition' in Moore's sense, where 'analytic' has its chemical connotation (analysis into constituents or components), and there is Moore's preferred view of philosophically proper definition, which is analytic in the semantic sense. There are lexical definitions, of the kind familiar in dictionaries, where approximating paraphrases do as well as the provision of synonyms. There is ostensive definition, which is actually a family of procedures of defining by showing, manifesting, displaying or demonstrating the definiendum, of which denotative definition – pointing a finger, perhaps while uttering the name of the thing picked out – is a focal case. There is definition in use, there is definition by paradigms (these differ technically from ostensive definitions because in order to grasp them the beneficiary of such definition must be able to extend application to relevantly like cases – the complexity of the procedure is considerable on the take-up side.) There are stipulative and abbreviating definitions, the latter in Russell's and Whitehead's *Principia Mathematica* sense. And all these are to be distinguished from – though they stand in close relation to – explication, description, analysis in the standard Russellian sense, and the tracing of connections between concepts as in the Strawsonian strategy.

Of these many kinds of definition Davidson considers only two, with the aim of rejecting them: definition by extensional paradigms, and what he describes as the 'definitional reduction' to simpler, clearer, and more basic concepts of the target concept. Now, this definition of definition is highly problematic. Russell insisted that definition and analysis are different, and that where a definition cannot be given, an analysis often can and should be.[17] And Russell meant by 'analysis' exactly what Davidson here means by 'definition': reduction to simpler, clearer, and more basic concepts. Russell contrasted analysis in this precise sense both with definition as he and Whitehead defined it in *Principia* and – for the cases he recognised as more germane to the treatment of problems outside the formal context – with definition as Moore understood it. The first kind is stipulative; it records a

---

17 Russell and Whitehead, *Principia Mathematica* (Cambridge: Cambridge University Press, 1910–12), Vol. I, p. 11.

decision to use symbols in a certain way. Moore's famous account focuses upon concepts; he rejects what, for present purposes, he confusingly calls 'analytic definitions', namely, definitions of *things* in terms of their parts and arrangements, as philosophically irrelevant. As to concepts, Moore requires that definitions should be analytic; definiens and definiendum must be synonymous if the former is to provide us with what we want in respect of the latter.

But for Russell an analysis breaks up and typically dissipates its target in the analysandum, so that it does not figure in the analysans. The lump of rock vanishes into a cloud of charged particles; the sentence with a definite description in grammatical subject place becomes a tripartite conjunction with, in the perfect language, bound variables in logically proper place: the definite description has vanished. So there is a sharp contrast between Russellian analysis and Moorean definition. Might it be that Davidson tacitly assumes Moore-leaning constraints in the reduction he has in mind as defining of definition? The fact that one has to ask suggests that we need a fuller account of what he takes definition to be; we cannot properly evaluate the claim that important concepts resist such definition until we have it.

Definition and analysis are however closely related, in a family whose other members include explication, description, classification, and what philosophers loosely call 'making sense' and 'giving an account'. It might be that these last two convey the inclusive notion, with the others as different members. In carrying on what James described as 'the dogged struggle to achieve clarity' we are accordingly not without resource, even if restricted to these. We should therefore be untroubled to find that *strict* and *precise* definitions, of the kind respectively possible in formal contexts and the natural sciences, are not generally available in contexts outside these. Certainly, few if any of the concepts important to philosophy admit of that kind of definition; irrespective of the exact nature of Davidson's understanding of definition, he is surely right about that.

But to say that such concepts cannot be *strictly* or *precisely* defined is not to say that they cannot be defined. The mistake arises from thinking that definitions must be definite. Think of the etymology of the term: to seek to define is to seek to find or –

just as importantly – to draw limits, to mark boundaries, to feel the edges of application. Often we have to negotiate and renegotiate these. A fuzzy boundary does not fail to be a boundary because it is fuzzy; we would have a very impoverished stock of general concepts if that were so.

The foregoing is intended to show that there is at best incompleteness and at worst a confusion at the root of Davidson's claim that it is folly to try to 'define' truth. If we bring this thought into conjunction with the remarks made earlier about Davidson's proposed alternative to 'definition' as he conceives it, one can go further. It is surely questionable, if it is an intended implication of Davidson's remarks, to hold that stating definitions (however conceived) and tracing conceptual connections exhaust the alternatives for philosophical method. For one thing, as suggested already, these are not mutually exclusive procedures. And apart from them – together with analysis and explication – there are a number of other characteristic vehicles of philosophy: for example, proof and argument, construction of theory, assembling reminders, persuasion, taxonomising, and criticism. It does not do to circumscribe, even by implication. So it seems that our ambition to get to grips with the important concepts of philosophy, not least among them truth – even to arrive at definitions of them in one of the many ways of definition – does not involve so much folly after all.

5

Concept-reference and natural kinds

In 'Putnam's Doctrine of Natural Kind Terms and Frege's Doctrine of Sense, Reference and Extension: Can They Cohere?' David Wiggins proposes placing Putnam's suggestions about natural kind terms into a Fregean framework of sense and reference, adjusting both Putnam and Frege in interesting ways in the process.[1] A consideration of these adjustments suggests to me, in turn, a way of defending an aspect of the kind of view about natural kind terms that Putnam and Wiggins are at one in rejecting. Let me make it clear that I am not defending the kind of view they reject: only one aspect of it, but a central one, having to do with the place of epistemic constraints on mastery of expressions in a language. If the relevant aspect of that view can be defended, it makes an important difference to the question of what conception of sense we can award ourselves if we agree, as we surely should, with those like Wiggins who argue that natural kind terms have sense.

To establish a point of approach I wish to begin with some considerations about a closely neighbouring matter. Recall briefly what 'Twin Earth' examples are alleged to illustrate. Familiarly, my twin and I drink, bathe in and make remarks about phenomenologically indistinguishable stuff we both call 'water', but on his earth the stuff so named has the chemical makeup XYZ whereas here it is

---

1 Wiggins, D., 'Putnam's Doctrine of Natural Kind Terms and Frege's Doctrine of Sense, Reference and Extension: Can They Cohere?' in A.W. Moore (ed.), *Meaning and Reference* (Oxford, 1993). At the 1992 Karlovy Vary conference my paper was a response to an earlier version of Wiggins's paper. Although at the conference Wiggins made some adjustments to his argument in his response to my response, the main points at issue remain eminently pursuable. I am grateful to Wiggins for discussion of them, then and since.

H₂O. Putnam took this to upset a brace of traditionally platitudinous theses about meaning, one being that meaning determines extension, the other that meaning is determined by the content of certain mental states of speakers (let us abbreviate the discussion required here by saying: speakers' knowledge and beliefs).[2] The Twin Earth case suggests that these traditional platitudes contradict each other, for the first implies that 'water' has a meaning in my twin's mouth different from the meaning it has in mine, while the second – granting the atom-for-atom identity of our twinhood and the determination of psychological states by states of central nervous systems – implies the opposite.

The usual responses to the Twin Earth dilemma consist in denials of or modifications to one or both the traditional platitudes. Enrich the first platitude by relativisation to context, and contradiction disappears. Or distinguish 'wide' from 'narrow' meaning: the first, extension determining; the second, restricted to what governs a speaker's use of an expression by being psychologically manifest for him in his grasp of it; and again, contradiction disappears. Or one could even adopt the currently unfashionable strategy of denying the second traditional platitude, by holding that mental states are not related to central nervous systems in the premised way. Here contradiction does not even threaten.

But questions about Twin Earth cases might arise at an earlier point. One gets drawn into discussing them only because one has already accepted certain theses about natural kind terms which load the dice against, in particular, any version or cognate of the second traditional platitude. Chief among them is the thesis that natural kind terms designate rigidly and in virtue of facts about the real natures of kinds of things – their essences – which need not and well might not be known to users of expressions designating them.

I have had occasion to argue elsewhere that this is a not entirely convincing doctrine. I rehearse just one of the considerations briefly. Recall Kripke's proposals about the nature of essence as internal structure.[3] 'Tigers', he says, 'cannot be defined simply in

---

2 Putnam, H., 'The Meaning of "Meaning"' in *Mind, Language and Reality* (Cambridge, 1975).

3 Kripke, S., *Naming and Necessity* (Harvard, 1980). For this response see Grayling, A.C., 'Internal Structure and Essence' in *Analysis* 1982.

terms of their appearance; it is possible that there should have been a different species with all the external appearances of tigers but which had a different internal structure and therefore was not the species of tigers.'[4] Note first that internal structures are nested: tigers have internal organs, these are composed of cells, which in turn are composed of molecules, in their turn composed of atoms, and so on down through elementary particles to so far merely hypothesised structures – 'superstrings' were a recently fashionable candidate – and perhaps beyond. Genes must count as a fairly high level of structure in this hierarchy. Now, suppose we ask which level of structure constitutes the essence. Suppose two tigers have the same structures all the way down to a certain level – say, the atomic – but differ thereafter. Which is the tiger? It could be replied, as a geneticist might reply, that all levels of structure are uniformly correspondent, so that similarity at any one of them entails similarity at all; this indeed is how geneticists justify identificatory claims about an individual's species based on investigation of small samples of its tissue. But why then should this correspondence not run up to the highest level of structure, namely external structure, so that it – that is, appearance – counts as sufficient for the determination of kinds? Kripke and Putnam reject this, but unless some level of internal structure is privileged as uniquely kind-determining, independently of whatever competing higher-level structures might supervene upon it, it is no longer clear why. In practice we rely on our theories about the genetic level in the case of living kinds; but that is not a resource in the case of elements like gold and stuffs like water; and anyway our doing so for living kinds does not settle the matter, it only starts the required debate about what counts as telling the difference between, on the one hand, correctly identifying the real natures of things, and on the other hand classifying them according to our own theoretical convenience and interests.

Further, if difference of structure entails difference of kind, a counterintuitive result follows, which is that each individual is its own kind. For every individual is unique – this tiger has longer claws than that one – and such differences result from differences

---

4 Kripke, *ibid.*, p. 156.

at more fundamental levels of structure, including those under-lying the chemistry of DNA. This disagreeable result can be blocked by saying that it is a logical sum of the internal properties which count, the sum of inclusive disjunction. Kripke and Putnam reject this for external structure, that is, appearance; Putnam allows only that this can enter into fixing a 'stereotype' of the kind in question; but here what gets disjoined are proper-ties which rarely if ever figure in stereotypes because they are much less accessible and far more theory-dependent than those which typically do.

Similar arguments can readily be adduced to unsettle us over other candidates for essence, for example 'origin'.[5] What they jointly suggest is that the notion of a natural kind, and hence of a natural kind term, is not well defined. It was Quine who taught us to be suspicious of claiming that our way of carving the world follows its joints; which must be a reason why he finds so bizarre the notion of essence, without which the notion of a natural kind is – perhaps insuperably – difficult to make clear.[6]

These thoughts in turn prompt a further: that ill-definition of the concept of natural kinds makes a difficulty for the view that correct use of natural kind terms does not depend upon what speakers know or do, but on the way the world is, independently of speakers. Note what this turns on: a commitment to the view that rigid designators, like air guns and golf balls, have correct uses but – because use and sense fall apart – no sense: the first platitude had it that sense determines extension, but on this view

---

5 Since all living things apparently derive from primeval slime, some node on the evolutionary tree will have to be selected as the place where, say, man's origin lies. Where is that? When one is selected, presumably on genetic grounds, the question already encountered becomes pressing: does this reflect our classifica-tory decisions, or the real nature of things? How do we tell which? And so forth.

6 There are other ways of making the point about the ill-definedness of the concept of natural kinds. One is to question whether designators of kinds are truly rigid (*cf.* W. A. Collins 'Types, Rigidity and A Posteriori Necessity' in *Midwest Studies* XII.) Another is to say that we may have variable concep-tions of kinds not dependent on essential facts; so XYZ might just be another sort of water, microstructural differences from H_2O notwithstanding (*cf.* Tim Crane, 'All the Difference in the World' in *Philosophical Quarterly* 41 (1991)).

extension, quite literally, determines itself: and on occasions of reference we proceed only with the help of the rule-of-thumb provided by something like Putnam's 'stereotypes' until the experts arrive. And even then – supposing we are ingenuously realist about their sciences, and that we leave aside questions about the inherent defeasibility of their theories and whether such theories are not irreducibly instrumental anyway – even then it cannot be guaranteed that the experts will know enough.

This view is, I suggest, to some extent destabilised by scepticism over kinds, essence and our ability to determine whether we are carving the world its way or ours. For it is hard to know what to do with a theory of a given sort of terms which is crucially dependent on a conceptually unsteady category of things, claimed to be often unknown and potentially unknowable, which the theory itself postulates and which putatively constitute the determiners of those terms' correct use.

I wish, however, to carry forward only two aspects of this thought to a discussion of Wiggins's proposals, given that, in contrast to Putnam's austerity of view, he embraces a notion of sense for natural kind terms. The ill-defined character of natural kinds is one aspect. The other is that it is at least deeply implausible – one is inclined to agree with a tradition stemming from Locke that it is impossible – that our employment of a term can be determined by something of which we are ignorant. In the framework of the traditional platitudes, this might be put as a requirement that the second of them – that what we know or believe enters constitutively into what our expressions mean (that what we mean by them enters into what they mean: a Griceful thought) – controls their relation to what they range over, at least as much as they are controlled by it in turn. This point is central in what follows later. At this juncture it need only be remarked that a large part of the pressure towards thinking this way comes from the reflection that just as it is intolerable to suppose that speakers are uninvolved in settling what the expressions they utter apply to, so it would be intolerable to countenance a third-realmist realism about senses which regards their objectivity as such that an expression may have a sense which no current user of the language attaches to it: that indeed an expression may have a sense which has, say, been forgotten and will never be recovered, and that speakers who attach a different sense to it are accordingly just mistaken.[7]

There is one more point I must mention before turning to Wiggins's account. At the outset of thinking about these matters, there is a natural enough hope that one might be able to give a univocal account of expressions having potentially predicative use, and it is a discovery of some moment, if discovery it is, that this is not so. In the case of natural and non-natural kind terms it may turn out that a univocal account of them is impossible precisely for Putnam's reason, that whereas one might be able to define the latter in terms of conditions which are both necessary and sufficient for their application, no such definitions are possible for the former. We are reminded here of a thought about grounds for attributing mastery to speakers in the case of colour terms, as an example of the cases of at least many general terms - not only characterising terms but sortals too. Plausibly, speakers may be credited with grasp of a colour term on the joint evidence of these three marks: that they recognise what counts as a focal case of the colour in question, that they consistently reject application of the term in focal cases of what is not that colour, and that they agree by and large with fellow-speakers in hesitating over application of the term on the indeterminate boundaries between that colour and its neighbours. It is open to us to suggest that mastery of natural kind terms is best understood in rather this way; that the chief difference between mastery of this sort and knowledge of necessary and sufficient conditions is degree of open-endedness of the concept in play; and that in both cases application of terms is epistemically driven in quite definite and straightforward ways. Once again, this point re-emerges in due course, and is by no means at odds with the modified Putnamian account Wiggins wishes to give.[8]

---

7 What prevents this from being the logically extreme consequence of holding sense and idea apart as Frege does?

8 It is worth wondering in passing whether or not on the Putnam-Kripke view of natural kind terms, it should be held that from the vantage point of an ideal epistemic agent (say, God), necessary and sufficient conditions for the application of any natural kind term can be given. Presumably so; which would make our account of natural and non-natural kind terms univocal, the apparent difference between them being merely a function of the ignorance

I turn now to Wiggins's view, which I describe and discuss in detail because I propose to define my own view by differing from it in what I shall argue are crucial ways at crucial points.[9]

For Wiggins the attraction of Putnam's theory of natural kind terms is that it attaches their meaning to the real natures of kinds by a *deixis*, a means of assignment by exemplification in which a term is attached to a kind under 'special and favourable' circumstances for conveying what it is about samples that can lead on to a richer grasp of the term's extension. Deixis is not to be understood so that natural kind terms are compared to index-icals or demonstratives; 'water' must not be compared to 'this'. Nor must it be understood as making mere ostension the key. The comparison Wiggins invites us to draw is, rather, to proper names, understood in terms of a view in which they have their meaning, and make their contribution to truth-conditions, by standing for their bearers; and in which the only way to give their senses is to say which objects they stand for.[10] Moreover, the senses of proper names are 'reality-invoking or object-involving', and have their senses 'by being assigned to something, not by the laying down of a specification such that a bearer of the name bears it by virtue of meeting that specification'.[11] The prospect held out by Putnam's proposal, Wiggins suggests, is that something very similar can be said in the case of natural kind terms.

In Wiggins's view the reason why philosophers found it diffi-cult to arrive at a deictic or extension-involving conception of meaning for natural kind terms was their conviction that, despite Quinean strictures, there could still be well-founded agreement on what counts as analytic. And accordingly they still found it

---

suffered by finite epistemic agents. This view indeed conforms neatly with the principle in traditional syllogistic that the difference between natural and non-natural kinds is that the former fall under an indefinite number of pred-icables (perhaps too many for us to know) and the latter under just one. Alex Orenstein suggested to me a different way of effecting the assimilation of the two kinds of kind-terms: since God made all the natural kinds, they are non-natural (artifact) kinds anyway, and this underwrites the univocality of the account to be given of both.

9 The version of Wiggins's paper referred to here was the one presented at the conference in Karlovy Vary with my paper as respondent.
10 Wiggins, p. 2.
11 *Ibid.*

possible to attempt analyses and to look for non-circular necessary and sufficient conditions. Putnam's proposal constitutes a
more moderate and effective second onslaught on analyticity. It
does not deny that definition by necessary and sufficient conditions can be given of single criterion concepts, but it refuses to
generalise from them. Once this point is taken, the possibility
offers of exploring the idea that there are 'sense-giving relations
between predicates and kinds that could mimic the direction of
fit we now take for granted in our understanding of the setting up
of the relation of designation'.[12]

Wiggins's aim is to show how the extension-involvingness of
natural kind terms coheres with the theory of sense and reference. He begins by glossing the diagram Frege drew for Husserl
in a letter of 24 May 1891. What he says about the middle column
is important because his account of concept-reference – the third
column – centres upon it.

Sentence	Singular Term	Concept-word	
Sense of the Sentence (Thought)	Sense of the singular term	Sense of the concept word	
Reference of the sentence, a truth value	Reference of the singular term, an object	Reference of the concept word, a concept	Object(s) that fall under the concept

The notion of the sense of a singular term is to be understood
in the light of Frege's remarks about fictional names. Frege says
that the name 'Nausicaa' has sense, in so far as it does, by behaving
as if it designates some girl. Wiggins takes this to license a simpler
claim for the non-fictional case: 'a name has sense by behaving as
if it has – or simply by having – a reference. A name has its sense
then by somehow presenting its object. To grasp the sense of a
name is to know (in the manner correlative with the mode of
presentation that corresponds to this somehow) which object the
name is assigned to.'[13] Taking the sense of a name as its mode of

---

12 Wiggins, p. 6.
13 Wiggins, p. 8.

presentation of an object means that we have two things here: an object that the name presents, and a way in which it is presented. This latter Wiggins calls the 'conception' of the object. This is 'a body of information' – typically open-ended and imperfect, and hence rarely if ever condensable into a complete description of the object – in which the object itself plays a role. We must be careful to insist on the open-endedness of conceptions in order to distance the account from one in which some description or set of descriptions of a thing is taken to be synonymous with its name. The most that we can reasonably expect is that the conception of something X to which the sense of X's name is 'keyed' might generate various descriptions of X which in suitable circumstances would help us to identify it. So:

Properly possessed then, the conception of an object X that sustains the sense of a name that is keyed to that conception is a way of thinking about X that fixes (with the help of the world, the world being what helps create the conception) which object the object in question is. Which object the object is, is precisely what is mastered by he who comes to understand the name with the sense corresponding to that conception.[14]

With these points made, Frege's third column is glossed by paralleling concept-words and singular terms. The parallel is claimed to be direct. Just as grasping the sense of a name and its contribution to truth-conditions is to grasp the conception – 'corresponding to the name's mode of presentation of what the name stands for' – of the object, and just as giving the name's sense is to say, 'in a manner congruent with that conception', what object it stands for, so grasping the sense of a predicate and its contribution to truth-conditions is to grasp its mode of presentation of the concept it stands for. Giving its sense is done by saying what concept it stands for. We demonstrate preferences for one sense over another by preferring one mode of presentation or body of information over another; examples of the two ways of expounding bodies of information about, say, horses, might be found respectively in a dictionary and a zoological textbook.[15]

---

14 *Ibid.*
15 Wiggins, pp. 8–9.

Thus armed Wiggins can anticipate concluding that Putnam's stereotypes approximate to the conceptions which sustain the senses of natural kind terms; stereotypes are 'particular special ways of thinking in identificatory fashion about such kinds and their specimens'.[16] But this is so far only an anticipation: there are adjuncts to the view that make a significant difference. These become manifest upon closer examination of the analogy between columns 2 and 3.

As the diagram makes clear, predicates do not refer to objects but to concepts. In his letter to Husserl, Frege points out that it takes one more step to reach an object from a concept-word than from a singular term, but that it may also happen that the concept word is scientifically useful even though the concept it refers to is empty. Thus his reason for putting objects off to the side in his diagram, but at a level with concepts to show that they share the same objectivity. Thus the thesis that predicates refer to concepts is wholly general, and neither brings out what is distinctive about natural kind terms nor what a theory like Putnam's makes of them. On Putnam's theory the point is that one has to be exposed to the extension of the term to acquire mastery of it; there is no grasping the reference or concept otherwise. Understanding cannot be acquired by grasping a 'strict lexical definition', for no such thing is available. 'So whereas the reality-involvingness of proper names amounts to their being reference-involving, the reality-involvingness of natural kind terms amounts to their being *extension*-involving.' And this permits us to say that what it is to have a grasp of say, the concept *horse* is to know that Red Rum and Arkle are horses, that is, to know the truth-conditions of 'Arkle is a horse'.

What is being welcomed in Putnam's account is the thought that natural kind terms can only be mastered deictically; specifying the concepts they refer to depends on giving examples. But Wiggins insists that this can only happen if what the speaker thereby acquires is a recognitional capacity, sustained by a 'conception' or body of information. In teaching a tyro a natural kind term what is imparted is just such an identificatory or recogni-

16 Wiggins, p. 9.

tional conception. It is this that corresponds to the sense of a natural kind term. What one must say then is that the sense of a natural kind term is correlative to a recognitional conception that is unspecifiable except as the conception of things like this, that and the other specimens exemplifying the concept that this conception is a conception of.[17]

In sum (taking the term 'horse' as example) the doctrine is 'that which supports the sense of the substantive "horse" is a certain identificatory conception of the concept *horse*'.[18]

A conception and a concept are of course different. A conception is a way of thinking about a concept (or about the objects falling under it). More to the point (and here is where Fregean and Putnamian considerations are merged) a conception is – with one important adjustment – a Putnamian stereotype. The adjustment is this. Recall that by 'stereotype' Putnam means, in Wiggins's formulation of the view, 'a fund of ordinary information or a collection of idealised beliefs that one needs to grasp in order to get hold of the meaning of a thing-kind word'. Now Putnam insists that the stereotypes and the extension of natural kind terms are quite independent. A speaker may have a stereotype for 'horse' but no knowledge of the extension; such knowledge is the preserve of experts. He supports this by laying celebrated claim to arboreal ignorance: I know the stereotype of elm and the stereotype of beech, he says, but I cannot tell them apart. One might naturally be sceptical about the segregation; there must be *some* link of the kind sketched earlier when conceptions were introduced. What we should hold is that a stereotype is the stereotype of a given concept, and that grasping the stereotype 'represents the beginning of an identificatory capacity ... which could *advance* to the point where it became the capacity of the expert'.

Changed emphases, and a few crucially located adjustments, yield a picture which differs from this otherwise attractive account in significant ways – not least, as suggested, in offering a theory of the sense of concept-words which respects epistemic constraints.

---

17 Wiggins, p. 12.
18 *Ibid.*

First I note that Wiggins accepts or at any rate does not question the view of natural kinds central to Putnam's account; in particular, he does not question how well-defined the notion is, and whether, as I gave reasons for thinking, it is in fact not so, and this because kinds themselves are not; and whether therefore the open-endedness of concepts of kinds, and the correlative impossibility of giving 'strict lexical definitions' of them, is a function of this fact. For Wiggins, it would seem, the imperfection of the bodies of information in which conceptions consist is a function of our ignorance about something that is, independently of us, quite objective and determinate, namely, the extension of the term whose sense that conception sustains. This view is opposed not just to anti-realist theses which might be variously nominalist or conventionalist about kinds (opposing the objectivity claim), but by versions of realism about kinds in which they are just not very neat (opposing the determinateness claim). The world, on such a view, might simply be genetically – or, more basically, chemically – ambiguous in ways that made kinds more like colours than like artefacts, most of which are completely determinate, a characteristic of non-natural kinds as the point about single-criterion applicability of their designators shows. Either on the anti-realist or realist possibilities here mooted, a difference is made to our understanding of kind terms.

Having registered these thoughts, let us leave them in the background for the present. The first foreground anxiety concerns conceptions and their relation to senses. There is something uneasy about this. A conception, recall, is a body of information. At first Wiggins says, in speaking of Frege's claim that a sense is a 'mode of presentation', that this involves the existence of two things: an object – the reference of the name – and a way the object is presented. But it immediately appears that the way the object is presented is not, as one would expect, the sense, but a conception, that is, a more or less rough body of information in which the object figures.[19] The move that troubles is that alongside 'sense of the singular term' in Frege's diagram, and off to one

---

19 This too raises a question: why not say directly that a conception is a body of information about the object? Perhaps Wiggins chooses the less committal formulation to insure against convergence with description theories of names.

side, we must make an additional entry; we must write 'conception'. The conception is more or less, in effect, what a cluster of descriptions is in the theory which equates such clusters with senses; but Wiggins keeps the two apart, and speaks of senses being 'keyed' to conceptions, or 'sustained' by them, or as 'corresponding' or being 'congruent' to them; and that we give a term's sense 'by saying in a manner congruent with that conception what the term stands for'.[20]

Both the relation and the difference between senses and conceptions is hard to specify. In the passage under consideration what troubles is the immediate move to saying that terms have both reference and sense but that what presents the reference to thought in a certain identificatory way is a third thing, the conception: 'To speak as Frege does of sense as "mode of presentation" suggests then nothing less than this: there is an object that the name presents and there is a way in which the object is presented, or a conception, as I shall say, of that object.'[21] Here 'modes of presentation' has shifted from being what senses are to being what conceptions are. Conceptions thereafter do all the work; they fix the reference ('with the help of the world'), present the object, and serve as what must be taught a tyro in his acquisition of mastery of the term.

It is clear that Wiggins is trying to preserve the advantages of something similar to a description theory of sense, for this makes a good marriage with Putnam's notion of stereotypes, while trying to avoid the disadvantages of equating the sense with a given body of information. But if the informational aspect of grasp of a term is hived off into a detachable package, namely the conception, what is there left for the sense to be? As it stands, Wiggins has dieted Frege's notion of sense to something blade-thin. A name's sense is what it stands for, 'congruent with the conception' of the object which 'sustains' that sense. It is clear that Wiggins seeks to avoid espousing a simple denotative theory in which the meaning of a name is the object it stands for, by having conceptions 'sustain' the relation of 'standing for' – to clothe the nakedness, so to say, of the denoting relation. But at the same time he

---

20 Wiggins, p. 8.
21 *Ibid.*

does not wish this package of information to *constitute* the sense, because that would be to espouse the equally questionable description theory. So he seeks to manoeuvre between the two by having something of both, held apart yet linked by the presence of the metaphorical relation of 'sustaining', 'corresponding', 'being congruent with'.

It is not a criticism of Wiggins to say that he is seeking some way of having the best of both sorts of view in a satisfying account of sense, for if he succeeds he provides a legitimate addition to the options. The problem lies with the vagueness of the relation between conceptions and senses. I asked: if conceptions are detachable packages of information, what is there left for senses to be? Whatever the answer to this question is, it will have in important part to turn on the nature of the relation between conceptions and senses. As long as that relation remains vague, so does the notion of sense. One is inclined to suspect that more express characterisations of the relation would let information bleed from conceptions into senses: which would call into question Wiggins's grounds for thinking that the relation between them is much short of identity.

A complication here is that it is anyway not clear whether the relation we are seeking to understand obtains between a one-to-one pair, a conception and a sense, or whether it is many-one, several conceptions correlating with a single sense.[22] One possibility is that sense is something minimal. The sense of a given designating term N consists in its having a given object X as its reference; the sense of N is 'that X is its reference'. Then if some other term M has X as its reference also, N and M have the same sense, *viz.*, that X is their reference; and what makes an identity statement 'N = M' informative, if it is so, is that they differ in the conceptions associated with them. As Frege's view is usually understood, what Frege meant by *Sinn* is in this respect at least similar to what on this construal is meant by 'conception'. However, Wiggins is as we know seeking to exploit Putnam's notion of a stereotype, a notion particularised to the case of natural kind terms; and this Putnamian notion is rather different from a notion of conceptions which can stand many-one to a

---

22 Michael Woods suggested this point to me in discussion.

Concept-reference and natural kinds

sense, for it would seem that there can only sensibly be one stereotype per natural kind term, since it is hard to see how a given stereotype for a given kind could properly serve as such if a *different* body of information could also serve as the stereotype for that kind. Given this, and because it is natural kind terms we are thinking about, at least in this case it would seem that Wiggins must or should think that there is one conception per sense; consistently with this interpretation he speaks throughout of the conception keyed to or sustaining the sense of a given natural kind term.

Either way, however, we are left with the difficulty that the relation between conception and sense is unclear, and that so also therefore is the notion of sense itself. These difficulties can be entirely avoided if we recognise that there is already a way of identifying senses and conceptions without inviting the difficulties inherent in theories like the description theory. Recall that a conception is a body of information, imperfect and open-ended, which can be extended to the point of expertise by refinement and accretion of information. But despite its imperfection and open-endedness, the conception – considered as Putnamian stereotype adjusted so as not to be independent of the extension – has to be such that it gives ordinary users of the term a mastery of it sufficient for the purposes, surely exigent enough, of ordinary communication. Possession of the conception-stereotype confers a capacity on the possessor to identify the reference of a term. Now, what is the objection to cutting through the multiplication of notions here by saying that this is what a term's sense is: an *open-ended, extensible body of information, possession of which enables speakers to identify the term's reference*? This keeps better faith with Frege's intentions, while not laying claim to the existence of a specific piece of information – some one description or cluster of them – which is the term's synonym.

What might be gained by thinking this way? Consider the most salient of facts about language. Because it is a public instrument of communication, for the functioning of which it is a necessary condition that senses be public and stable, it follows that the bodies of information in which, on this view, senses consist must be shared by users. On Putnam's view a stereotype is a *core* of information, which implies a minimum basis for mastery.

Wiggins adopts this for conceptions, noting that beyond it there is a large area for additions up to expert level. There seems to me no more difficulty in holding that the shared public sense of a term can be given as the open-ended core of information required for identifying its reference, than there is in requiring as much of Putnam's stereotypes or Wiggins's conceptions. This is exactly what dictionaries and entries in reference works do.

The point can be explicated as follows. In saying what is involved when a tyro is taught a natural kind term, and arguably any designating expression, it would be implausible to hold that the act of fixing the reference of the term for him stops short there, for this is to hold that there can be such a thing as *bare baptismal knowledge* of the reference of a term, possession of which is all that mastery of the term need consist in. For in coming to identify something X as the reference of N the tyro acquires information and beliefs about X beyond the mere fact that N designates it; information and beliefs of just the sort Wiggins has in mind as conferring a recognitional capacity. It would be bizarre to hold that when Fred tells Joe 'this is a tiger, and so is that', and so on in the manner of giving Joe a conception for 'tiger', that Joe thinks, believes or conceptualises nothing further about the individuals so named and the collection to which they are thus asserted to belong. Indeed the fullest way to reconstruct Joe's musings as Fred teaches him to talk about tigers is surely to describe them as amounting to something like this: 'so, these large striped meat-eating four-footed growling animals are called "tigers"'. (I say 'to reconstruct fully' because Joe might, say, be too young to put matters just this way. But this is more or less what he has to know when he knows what he is talking about when he is talking about tigers.) In so musing, Joe has the correctable and extensible makings of something, knowledge of which relates *that* word in his language to *those* things. That something I am calling the 'sense'. Further, if it really is a grasp of the term he can thus be credited with, what he has is therefore what all competent users of the language have, for only then are he and they in communication.

Espousers of theories in which there is no more to be said about designating expressions, in this connection, than that such-and-such is sufficient for fixing their references, fail to take into account certain complexities which attach to them in different ways. In the case of a natural kind term, use of it has to be understood in a twofold way: concatenated with an article or demonstrative, it is used to refer to members, *qua* individuals, of a kind; but it is also understood that a certain relation obtains between individuals so referred to, which significantly groups them together; the relation being some kind of relevant similarity. One can see a case for saying that such notions as 'relevance' and 'similarity' are irreducibly epistemic, and that therefore the senses of such terms have fairly rich graspable descriptive content from the outset. But even if it were held that the relevant similarities in virtue of which individuals collect into kinds are recognition-transcendent, it remains the case that speakers have to be able to identify individuals, and identify them as members of their kind, in virtue of the (perhaps unknown) basis for this grouping, from which definite entailments follow, to govern what speakers can say and do in related connections. So here too we have cause for thinking that built into the senses of such expressions is what 'stereotypes' or 'conceptions' are claimed to do for users of them.

My first suggestion, then, is that the sense of a term is what Wiggins describes as a conception, and that there is therefore no reason to multiply entries in Frege's diagram by having 'conception' pencilled alongside 'sense'. But this is not to suggest that there is any straightforward parallel between the second and third columns in Frege's diagram; as some questions prompted by Wiggins's account suggest, matters may be otherwise.

The most obvious first thought is that when a parallel between singular terms and natural kind terms is mooted, what first springs to mind is that this will have natural kind terms designating *kinds*, suitably hypostatized to rank alongside the middle column's objects. But no suggestion is made that in addition to individual tigers the world contains this extra object, the kind *tiger*. Rather, what a natural kind term refers to is the concept of a kind. Now Frege is able to keep his diagram neat, and to have concepts as references in the third column, because he treats them as having the same objectivity as the objects which fall under them when any do. But two difficulties which immediately press are these: are we clear about what we are committed to if we go along with Frege's ontology of concepts, relations and functions?; and, if we make an independent assessment of the comparative statuses of, say, a tiger (the beast out there in the jungle) and our ordinary concept of a tiger, are we happy to regard whatever parallels as subsist between the expressions respectively designating them as direct?

We have at least been alerted by Dummett to the difficulty of pressing analogies between singular terms and concept-words too far.[23] The sense in which in Frege's view the latter can be said to have reference, granting already that the existence of concepts (relations and functions) commits us to admitting second-order quantification, is one in which, says Dummett, 'the notion of reference does not play the same role in regard to them as it does in regard to proper names'.[24] What is crucial in understanding predicates, relational terms and functional expressions is, familiarly and respectively, being true of an object, holding between objects, and yielding given values for given arguments. If one thinks of reference in terms not of its semantic role – that is, in terms of contribution to truth-conditions – but of an identification of the reference of an expression with its bearer, as in the prototypical case of naming, then the claim that predicates refer simply looks implausible.[25] The adapted Putnamian account of natural kind terms under consideration is based on an analogy with this latter aspect of reference, the relation of a name to its bearer. Perhaps this is the source of at least one of the worries it prompts.

A discussion of the complexities thus uncovered can be shirked if we leave Fregean exegesis aside and simply ask what is the least that we can allow as constituting grasp of a predicate term. And here we are helped by the thought that to understand a predicate term is at least to know how to apply it: grasp of its sense is grasp of a criterion of application for it, the core capacity thus provided being an ability to judge the truth-value of basic predications effected by its means. More may well be required, depending on the kind of predicate in question; but we should find it hard to attribute to a speaker grasp of the sense of any such term which did not endow him with at least this.[26] In turn, this

23 Dummett, *Frege: Philosophy of Language* (2nd ed.) (1981), chapter 7, *passim*.
24 *Ibid.*, p. 245.
25 *Ibid.*, pp. 210–11.
26 *Ibid.*, p. 233. Dummett brings out, e.g., the difference between common nouns and adjectives as to ingredient criteria of application and identity.

suggests that what is to be grasped crucially about their senses is what it is for them to apply to or be true of items of suitable types. Taking Wiggins's notion of a body of information again, we might say that the sense of a concept-word is the core information we must have to enable us to apply it in exemplary cases – more generally put, perhaps: to recognise the truth-values of sentences in which such expressions occur on exemplary occasions. The 'exemplary' here shows that we are keeping faith with the idea of the openness of senses to addition and development to expert levels, while at the same time respecting the constraint represented by the demand that speakers share a core grasp of senses if language is to work as a public instrument of communication.

To this we can add a further point. Theories of sense typically underestimate or ignore the creative ability of speakers to grasp rules for the use of terms in new or variant applications. This is not a merely empirical claim; it exploits another requirement for the possibility of language, namely, that since speakers have to learn language for severely practical purposes, and with finite capacities in a limited time, and moreover since vagueness and open-endedness are essential properties of many expressions and their senses respectively, it is clear that it is a necessary condition for the existence of language that speakers should be able to extrapolate correct uses from sample cases. It is therefore no surprise that senses may have the open-ended character here attributed to them. So we can specify that a learnability condition has to apply as adjunct to the publicity condition just sketched, and that for this, senses have to have the character here claimed.[27]

These thoughts do not amount to a theory of the senses of concept words in general; perhaps they approach the identification of constraints to be respected in the construction of one. But even as such they entail a redrawing of the third column in Frege's diagram, and at very least to the weakening of the analogy between the second and third columns which Wiggins finds attractive for the case of natural kind terms. Since the task of offering the detail of a positive alternative theory is not to the point here, just one remark is pertinent: it is that on the mini-

---

27 This aspect of grasp of sense may contain materials for dealing with the problems which, Wiggins acknowledges, infect deixis: *cf.* p. 4.

mum specification given for the grasp of the sense of a concept word, any concept word which applies to nothing retains its sense because what is known by one who understands it is what would count as an exemplary instance of its application if ever one offered. This at least squares with Frege's view that concept-words which refer to empty concepts can still be useful, even scientifically so. And it also squares with the thought that one should treat the reference of concept words primarily in the semantical sense – as explaining how such words contribute to the truth-conditions of sentences in which they figure – and not on that aspect of the analogy with singular terms in which the reference of a term is identified with its bearer.

Wiggins remarked that it is distinctive of natural kind terms that a necessary condition for grasping their senses is exposure to their extensions. Such grasp, Wiggins insisted, cannot be acquired by means of a 'strict lexical definition'. This second point has already been embraced; it seems not merely right but crucial to an understanding of the notion of sense for such terms that they be taken as open-ended and approximate. But what is rejected here is not the idea of a lexical definition, but the idea of strictness. For it is clear that talk of 'exposure to the extension of natural kind terms' cannot be taken to be a demand that only those who have been to the zoo or had an adventure in the jungle grasp the sense of 'tiger'. As we would colloquially say, I know the meaning of many kind words despite not having been perceptually exposed to individual members of those kinds; a grateful example is 'rattle-snake'. But if exposure to the extension of such terms can mean the kind of lexical definition which conveys core information and thus a recognitional capacity for exemplary cases, while leaving open further and variant possibilities, then there can be no cavil over 'exposure'. Generalising from natural kind terms, we might wish to say that concept words which, in Frege's terminology, refer to empty concepts, can nevertheless be understood, because we can be (so to say) lexically exposed to – it is more accurate to say: given an understanding of what it would be for something to fall into – the extensions they would, in better or fuller worlds, have.

A point for Wiggins's proposals here is this: on Frege's view we can grasp the senses of concept words which lack extensions.

Wiggins points out that it is distinctive of natural kind terms, a subclass of concept words, that exposure to the extension is a necessary condition for grasp of them. So a further divergence between Wiggins's diagram and Frege's appears: the account of concept words is not univocal. This is not by itself a criticism, merely an observation. But note that if we accept Wiggins's analysis it makes natural kind terms more like singular terms than other concept words are. So perhaps natural kind terms should appear in a fourth column intermediate between the second and third on Frege's diagram. This emendation to the scheme is a function of realism about natural kinds, expressing itself through the demand that the extension be integral to the determination of sense (on Wiggins's view, via conceptions). But now recall the anxiety over the well-definedness of natural kinds and hence terms designating them. Suppose for a moment that the way we carve up the world is a response not to its contours but to our capacities and interests, and that therefore kinds are conceptual artefacts. Then natural kind terms are concept words; and may refer to empty concepts; and the account to be given of them and their senses is the same as for concept words in general. Then no fourth column needs to be added to Frege's diagram. We get a univocal and hence more economical account, we avoid problems over the doubtful aspects of natural kind theory – and even if everything realists assume about natural kinds turns out to be true, our theory would still explain how we grasp, as manifestly we do, the senses of expressions used in talk of them. This view is less committal than Wiggins's, and makes no ontological assumptions about natural kinds; so even if the view of natural kinds that Wiggins assumes turns out to be true, this theory is saved as part of the stronger theory that would result.

But explanation in terms of core conceptions or stereotypes – just as for concept words which refer to empty concepts – of how natural kind terms have publicly shared senses, is not going to be made somehow more adequate by adding to 'this is how to recognise an X if there are any' the clause 'and there really are some!' This extra fact does not make one understand more or better what X is. Wiggins took it that the extension-involvingness constraint ensured the realism of the reality-involvingness he took this to entail: these thoughts show he is wrong.

Perhaps the point which will be least congenial to some in this response to Wiggins is the invocation of a notion of sense which says that natural kind terms have senses consisting in describable informational content which, as grasped by speakers, is what presents the terms' references to them in a way that is common to at least the very great majority of such speakers. I iterate the point that Wiggins is surely right in arguing that whatever information a speaker needs to acquire mastery of such a term, it must be correctable and extensible, and that ordinary employment of the term differs from expert employment only in degree – in quantity of knowledge or theory – not in kind. But to this must be added the condition that whatever information does the trick in giving a learner mastery of the term, that information must be the same as, or at the minimum must mesh with, the information guiding any other ordinarily competent user of the term. If such information constitutes sense, then the point is to be put by saying that senses must be public (Frege talks more strongly of senses being 'objective'). The modality here is straightforward: senses must be public, shared and relatively stable because language is an instrument of communication, and it is a necessary condition of its existence as such that at very least the great majority of speakers understand the same thing by the same expressions at the same time.[28] This means that something stabilises senses; that something counts as – at any one time – authoritative, despite long-term changes, as an account of an expression's meaning. This authoritative or standard sense of an expression is the product of agreement in use between speakers, and is what gets reported by lexicographers when they write their dictionaries. It is for this reason that, as we have all noticed from time to time, dictionaries are so useful. It is also for this reason that we are prepared to defer, when it comes to improvement of our grasp of natural kind terms, to those who are most informed in their uses of them.[29]

---

28 See my 'Publicity, Stability, and "Knowing the Meaning"', ch. 6 below.
29 I am grateful to those at Howard Robinson's summer vacation meeting group in Oxford, especially Alex Orenstein, Michael Woods, Howard Robinson, Anita Avramides, Michael Lockwood, John Foster, and Michael Martin, for their comments.

6

Publicity, stability, and 'knowing the meaning'

According to an influential view, meanings are not in the head. I wish to argue that although this is correct, meanings are nevertheless in our heads. No paradox is here intended: the plural possessive hints at the direction of argument.

To see this we have only to assemble certain reminders. I do not much disagree with those whose views I discuss; it seems to me that relatively minor adjustments of emphasis give us a perspective to prefer. But in the process we shall see that interesting twists are given to the usual tales told in this connection.

I approach matters by a familiar route, as follows.

One reason why it seems hard to get a satisfactory account of meaning is the apparent (but only apparent) conflict between two intuitions about language. One is that reference to certain facts about language-users seems to be ineliminable from any explanation of how semantic properties can attach to given arrays of sounds and marks, thereby constituting them as natural language. The other is that, given certain facts about the point of language, it seems necessary that, in important part, those very same properties should attach to those sounds and marks independently of the facts about language-users in question.

The problem is familiar enough. It exists in suitable variants both in meaning-theory and in the debate about mental content in general, the forms it assumes adapting itself to occasion. For my purposes the following is a convenient description of it. Sounds and marks abound in the world, but only some of them constitute natural language. Which ones? Those, it seems irresistible to say, animated by the intentions of their makers to communicate by their means – not just facts, but attitudes, desires, feelings, and the rest.[1] This thought is what motivates

For note 1, see next page.

intention-based semantics of Grice's sort – although it need not, as we shall see, by itself force us to reduce the semantic to the psychological, as Schiffer puts it, if we find its central intuition compelling.[2] But although we might not go the lengths of reduction, we might still take the intuition seriously, and accept that certain psychological facts have to be accorded a central place in any account of meaning.

On the other hand, the fact that language is an instrument of communication immediately introduces constraints that appear to conflict with this thought. Given that language is such an instrument, the senses of its component expressions have to be public and stable: *public* in the sense that different speakers of normal competence must generally understand the same things by the same expressions, that is, individuate meanings in conformity with each other; and *stable* in the sense that most expressions must retain over time the meanings they are publicly understood to have, and that the changes in meanings that naturally occur in the historical evolution of a language's expressions must not be so many, so rapid or so widespread as to render the language ineffective as a means of communication.

The appearance of conflict is sharpened when we raise either of two not unconnected psychological points. One concerns privacy; the other, the question whether psychological properties are to be understood narrowly – that is, as specifiable independently of facts about anything other than themselves, to which, when any relation between them subsists, they are therefore only externally related. The privacy point has it that a psychological state is accessible, and then only indirectly, to someone other than its possessor only if the latter reports or displays its content; but no-one other than its possessor can be in that state, only – when sympathy is great enough – in one like it: there can only be qualitative, never numerical, identity of states relating two or more subjects. One would expect narrow states to be private, but in the

---

1 Even in the performance of linguistic acts like persuading, soothing, marrying, promising, etc., there is communicated content at least in the close offing, readily inferable in standard cases.
2 Schiffer, *Remnants of Meaning* (Cambridge, Mass.: MIT Press, Bradford Books, 1987).

interests of publicity of meaning among other things, we might hope that the broad states of different subjects, in virtue of their internal connection to the same (numerically the same) objective relata, are less so, or in the ideal not so. An empirical consideration obtrudes, however: linguistic competence varies, and normally competent speakers not uncommonly mistake words, so the – so to speak – narrow end of broad states, the end constituting the speaker's own knowledge of meaning, plays an irreducible part in our problem. This thought indeed is a premise in the twin-earth argument which purports to show that meaning is not exhausted by speaker's meaning. Nevertheless, the central contribution made by speaker's knowledge remains at the narrow end.

In the presence of these points a summary statement of our problem comes to look like this: the meanings of expressions in language have to be public and stable so that language can be an instrument of communication; but meanings have in important part to be in the head. Note that, so far, merely stating the terms of this apparent conflict does not involve commitment to a theory about one side of the conflict whose rejection would be premissed by those who defend the other. For example: I take it that, say, Putnam and Burge would agree that *some* facts about what goes on in the heads of speakers are pertinent to questions of meaning.[3]

Does the conflict, as described, constitute a genuine problem? Few, I think rightly, would think so. To see why, one need only – as mentioned – assemble suitable reminders. It matters that we begin by getting clear about the publicity and stability constraints, to see how far their objectifying, and hence anti-individualistic, tendencies take us. And here a useful starting-point is afforded by Frege.

A major concern for Frege in arguing for the strong objectivity of sense is to detach questions about sense from those about anything peculiar to an individual mind when it grasps or employs an expression. Since sensations and images are wholly subjective, as are the mental processes in which grasping and employing a sense

---

3 The questions to which their respective views give decided answers are: which facts, and in what way are they pertinent?

consist, they are to be sharply contrasted to *what* is grasped in the course of thinking or to what sensations and images might accompany grasp of a sense, even when they accompany it invariably. 'A thinker stands', says Frege, 'in no comparable proprietary relationship to his thought, as the imaginer to his image. A thought is related in the same way, and as the same thing, to everyone who apprehends it.'[4]

Frege's robust commitment to objectivity of sense has a cluster of motivations, of which, for present purposes, the most salient is the desire to secure for senses a guarantee of their publicity. If senses were even only in part constituted by individually subjective associations they would fail to meet the stringent requirement Frege imposes: the sense of an expression has, he says, to be 'exactly the same for all rational beings, for all who are capable of apprehending it'.[5]

Implications to a third realm ontology need not concern us; as there are more ways than one of skinning a cat, so there might be more than one way to explain what strongly objective senses are. But the question is whether one has to go as far as strong objectivity to ensure that normally competent speakers generally understand the same by the same expressions; for although this might be the least that language requires to be a public instrument of communication, it is also arguably the most that one can expect. One reason is that when publicity and Frege's strong objectivity coincide, complete stability follows: nothing that any individual language user does, or even the community of them together, can corrode or vary an expression's meaning. But here empirical facts again obtrude: it is common for expressions to change in meaning over time. And this means that publicity must be something less than strong objectivity.

A yet more forbidding challenge is posed by learnability requirements. It is not easy to see how to begin an account of language-learning if sense is in some literal way third-realmish; but even the task of explaining acquisition on the weaker view that sense is independent of the knowledge or capacities of speakers, or their employments of the physical vehicles of sense (sounds and

---

4 Frege, 1983b, p. 145.
5 Frege, 1983a, p. 7.

marks), poses familiarly daunting difficulties, and we know that other tales thereby hang.[6] I leave them hanging; it suffices to remark one cognate point. The notion that sense is strongly objective in Frege's way entails that an expression (even an entire language) could mean something that no current speaker of the language knows. There could be expressions with senses which have been forgotten – perhaps they are now wrongly grasped, or lie dormant. Strongly objective sense is transcendent sense, and makes the highly counterintuitive demand on us to accept an absolute divorce between sense and use entailing the truth of sentences like this: 'such and such an expression means *m*, but no-one knows or can now discover what *m* is'.

What makes this demand counterintuitive is the thought, familiar almost to the point of platitude, that what is meant by what we say is at least in important part what we mean by what we say – just the Gricean thought weighing on one side of the apparent conflict under discussion. It is the intuition that use and intention are each at least part-determiners of meaning that is violated by strong objectivity. Just as the stability of meanings is a measure of speakers' needs in crucial respects, so their instability is a mark of their determination by what speakers do and intend. There are mutual constraints here: language serves its employers' needs by being bendable to their wills – but not too far, since over-plasticity would defeat the object in view, which is communication. Even so, the implication of the first conjunct is that publicity cannot be Fregean objectivity.

One reason why Frege goes too far is that – in distinguished company as we shall see – he commits the fallacy of composition. Publicity requires that neither I nor you, taking us individually, can be like Humpty Dumpty and mean what we like by our words; but the independence from me or you of the meaning of our words does not entail their independence from what the language-using community does with them. Use-theorists say: when enough of us use an expression a certain way, that is what it means; that is what lexicographers report when giving us a

---

6 Here is indicated one family of arguments against taking a 'realist' conception of truth to be pivotal for understanding meaning.

definition. The claim prompts us to suspect that since we can get publicity of meaning from intersubjectively constrained conformities of use, Fregean objectivity, even if it were plausible, is unnecessary.

We can now export these points to the current debate. Here interesting developments are in progress: we talk in one breath now of 'mind and language' and find it impossible to extricate considerations about one from the other, because we see that what we say about meaning, in particular about reference and the part played in it by sense, is so closely related to what we say about intentionality that we cannot consider them apart. Yet a consequence of emphasising anti-individualistic considerations – in respects to be identified, surely plausible – is to drive a wedge between language and mind, by promoting the independence of semantics from psychology. This restates the apparent conflict at issue.

The thought that premises anti-individualistic arguments is that the meaning of many expressions must be dependent on more than what is in the head of a speaker using it.[7] Originally the point was made in connection with the references of natural-kind terms, but the permitted generalisation is to the claim that 'the meanings of many terms – and the identities of many concepts – are what they are even though what the individual knows about the meaning or concept may be insufficient to determine it uniquely'.[8] The conclusion is that meanings[9] have to be 'broad', that is, at least in part constituted by factors outside the heads of language-users – 'environmental factors' as Burge calls them.[10]

In Putnam's view the conclusion to be drawn from this premise is, famously, that 'meanings just ain't in the head'.[11] Neither he

---

7 I take anti-individualism in Burge's sense, as the view that mental states and process cannot be type-individuated independently of facts about the individual's environment. In the case of meaning, the view is that meaning cannot be wholly a matter of what a speaker thinks or knows, but is dependent on what the expression applies to (in the case of reference, for example, to the extension; *cf.* Putnam).

8 Burge 'Philosophy of Language and Mind' in *Philosophical Review*, 1992, p. 46.

9 I should say: 'many meanings' – I ignore certain classes of expressions like indexicals and syncategorematic terms.

10 *Ibid.*

11 'The Meaning of "Meaning"' in *Philosophical Papers*, Vol. 2.

nor Burge go all the way with Frege to strong objectivity, so this slogan cannot be taken to mean all it appears to mean. Here then is a complaint: neither Putnam nor Burge locate for us the point on the spectrum of anti-individualism which, although falling short of strong objectivity, extends meanings beyond the head in the required way. Burge talks of the 'individual's physical or social environment' as what individuates the meanings of terms he employs, not alone but in 'deep individuative relation' to the individual's (relevant) mental states.[12] Putnam likewise does not claim that no part of the story about meaning refers to psychological states; his concern is to emphasise connections between them and something additional as constitutive of meaning. So far so good; but in both cases the claim is still too strong – in part for the same reason as in Frege's case – because it does not suitably restrict the extra-cranial aspect of meaning. Once again the mutuality of the constraints is in play: understanding publicity helps here too. The publicity requirement is one main motivation for treating meaning broadly, but if publicity is distinguished from strong objectivity, and something like the use-theorists' vague account of intersubjectively constrained conformities of use is to be helpful in its place, more detail is required.

Let us rehearse the argument showing that language is *essentially* public. This is a demonstration of two points: that language has to be learned in a public setting, and that criteria for correct use of expressions consists in the reciprocal government which speakers exercise over each others' linguistic performance, thereby promoting conformity. It is an argument which, despite its initial Wittgensteinian appearance, will not be found in Wittgenstein, because in the form it is offered here it runs against some of the received wisdom about private language and rule-following; but there are at least similarities to some of what Wittgenstein seems to say. It goes as follows.

It is not possible for there to be a language with just one speaker, not even in the sense of a contingently private language, because language is a rule-governed activity – to speak a language is to follow the rules for the use of its component expressions – and a

12 Burge 'Philosophy of Language and Mind' in *Philosophical Review*, 1992, p. 47.

speaker can only be following the rules if he is able to distinguish between doing so and only thinking he is doing so. This, in turn, he is only able to do if something independent of his own grounds for thinking he is doing so is available. What is required is an independent check on his observances, from a source which recognises the complex of rule, practice and any divergence of the latter from the former, for what it is. This premise is vital, and – incidentally – unWittgensteinian, because it imputes to interlocutors *understanding* of what a rule requires in the cases it governs. So it merits iteration: what is required is an independent check which recognises any divergence of practice from rule for what it is.[13] Accordingly it is not facts about the domain over which language ranges that can be appealed to in settling conformity with the rules, even for the simplest cases where a rule is, say, taught in connection with a referential term by ostension to paradigmatic samples of the extension, together with an account of how to go on later. Rather, the constraint has to come from another or others in the speaker's own situation, that is, other rule-followers. As in Wittgenstein's version of the argument, the constraint is therefore provided by a speaker's being one among others. From this the points to be demonstrated follow. Acquiring the language is acquiring competence in observing its constitutive rules, so language learning has to happen, as language-use has to continue, in a public setting. This means that language can never be even contingently private, because it could never get started, and if *per impossibile* it did, it could never go on.[14] Crispin Wright, and in some lights Wittgenstein also, think that language can be contingently private; Wright argues that the lifelong solitary islander who masters a Rubik's cube washed up on his beach, is a contingently private rule-follower. But this cannot be right if the key thought is that there must be something available to the islander, but independent of his own grounds for distinguishing between following a rule and only thinking he is doing so, which constrains his practice. So it will not do to say:

---

13 *Cf.* A. C. Grayling, 'Meaning, Mind and Method' in A. Phillips Griffiths (ed.), *Wittgenstein: Centenary Essays* (Cambridge, 1991).

14 Pepys's diary, and other examples of secret codes, are examples of public language in cipher, not 'contingently private languages'.

his observance of the rules could in principle be checked if others were by. Following a rule as opposed to thinking that one is doing so, or by accident doing so, is a strictly practical matter, and cannot be sustained by this kind of counterfactual. Let us take the modalities seriously: if a language cannot be contingently private, it must be essentially public; and this is what was to be shown.

Among other things, the argument not only helps unpack the notion of publicity itself, but thereby provides an answer to the question: where on the anti-individualistic spectrum, short of strong objectivity, is publicity located? Earlier it was suggested that some notion of intersubjectivity was as much as was needed for publicity, thus rendering Frege's strong objectivity unnecessary even were it plausible. Now it is clearer what this implies, for if publicity is *essentially* a matter of speakers' mutual constrainings of use, then intersubjective agreement of the right sort is not only as much as is either needed or available, but also the least that is required, for publicity. And this means that publicity of sense and intersubjective agreement in use coincide.

For espousers of one theoretical viewpoint, of course, this conclusion is already a commonplace. But arriving at it by this route shows us how to deal with the anxiety, left pending a few paragraphs ago, about Putnam and Burge. For they both seem to take it that the broad context required for meaning is something more than the shared activities of the speaker community. Largely because of the examples – talk of water and arthritis – which drive their views, they have it that broad context involves a realm of physical referents constituting a domain over which language ranges, and which exists independently of what is said about it. The domain's independence of language is required because it is facts about what it contains which settle what a speaker means, as the twin-earth case purports to show, given that what is narrowly in an individual's possession is insufficient for the task.

Two steps towards clarification are required here. First it is noteworthy that the move from 'independent of the individual speaker' to 'independent of language' or, more accurately, of speakers collectively considered, is just assumed; but as we saw earlier this is a version of the composition fallacy, and the claim that meaning depends upon something which is independent of the language and its users, taken collectively, is far stronger than the claim that what is in the narrow possession of an individual speaker is insufficient to determine an expression's meaning. Serious questions are already in the air because we have a compelling argument which says that language is essentially an inter-subjective product; we now have to ask whether there has to be an additional argument saying something stronger still, namely, that it is a further essential property of language that its speakers must occupy an environment which is at least in part physical. Put the question like this: imagine a community of disembodied minds occupying a non-physical realm. Are its members logically barred from being language-users because there is no physical environment to provide the broad context for meaning – that is, because the broad context is not more than a realm for the extensions of referring terms to occupy independently of what speakers, taken individually, know, but (more strongly) is such a realm because its denizens have *specifically physical* properties?

Recall Burge's claim that a speaker's mental states have to be deeply related to his 'physical or social environment' for the individuation of meaning. So far, the publicity considerations require of us only that the environment should be social, that is, that a speaker has to be a member of a community of speakers. The disjunction cannot stand without supplementation; if the environment has to be physical also, we need an argument to show us why. And there is of course some such argument, or what might be some such argument, in Putnam, given for the case of terms which refer to natural kinds, but extendable to any other classes of terms which plausibly take the same analysis.

Here are the relevant reminders. Putnam challenged two assumptions of hitherto received semantics, the first being that to know the meaning of an expression is to be in a certain sort of psychological state, and the second being that the meaning of an expression determines its extension. These assumptions entail that psychological states determine the extension of terms. Putnam's twin-earth case purports to show that this cannot be so, thus yielding the celebrated conclusion about meanings and the head. Of course this applies just when the psychological states in question are narrow, that is, understood in accordance with 'methodological solipsism', the view that psychological states supervene on intrinsic states of an individual considered independently of anything besides, in particular without relation to environmental factors causing or being effected by those states.

The first thing to note is that rejection of methodological solipsism does not by itself entail some kind of physical realism about the domain of application of the terms whose meanings are to be understood broadly. For so far all that we have identified as required in addition to the speaker's knowledge of meaning is the existence of other speakers whose interactions with him and one another constrain that knowledge. If this is not enough to serve as the broad context, then we need to find the reason in Putnam's twin-earth argument. Does his argument show that unless there is H_2O and XYZ out there on earth and twin-earth respectively, Oscar and his twin could not respectively have meant 'water' and 'water'? That of course is not what Putnam sought to conclude: his argument was not aimed at proving the existence of the external world, but at showing that meanings cannot be individuated narrowly. The existence of water H_2O and water XYZ is assumed, as is the qualitative identity of the twins' narrow states, together with their woeful ignorance of theory. Thus richly equipped, the argument has no difficulty in delivering its conclusion. But before we accept these premises in hastening to embrace that conclusion, we should enquire whether the twin-earth tale could not be as well or better told, because more parsimoniously told, using what we already have in addition to the individual's knowledge of meaning, *viz.*, the linguistic community's knowledge of meaning.

Any individual's problem is that he does not know everything that all other speaker's jointly know about the meaning of the expressions in his language. This is unsurprising: if some best and latest dictionary pooled a community's knowledge of meanings, it would be a rare individual whose linguistic knowledge came close. Such a dictionary would report the knowledge possessed by the completest speakers, including, for example, that of chemists and hydroengineers. Now let us postulate an 'Explicit Speaker', who knows everything in the best dictionary.[15] In knowing the

---

15 An exploration of the uses to which the notion of a 'Explicit Speaker', properly defined and developed, can be put, is to be found in my paper 'Explicit Speaker Theory', ch. 7 below.

meaning of 'water' he therefore knows that, in the latest state of chemical theory on earth, it is stuff of molecular structure H_2O. Let us suppose his twin-earth twin is equally encyclopaedic. Then he knows that 'water' according to twin-earth chemistry is XYZ. What has happened? Well, in the idealised state of knowledge of meanings – that is, where an individual speaker has at his disposal the linguistic community's best joint knowledge – we find that when he says 'water' he intends to refer to water, that is, H_2O, or if he lives on twin-earth, then to water on twin-earth, that is, XYZ; and so in either case his grasp of the expression's meaning determines its extension, and the psychological state in which his grasp of the meaning consists is broad. But this is not because it is related, causally or in some other way, to water, but rather to theories about water, because he is speaking in conformity with the best dictionary, that is, with the fullest available knowledge of meanings, in accordance with the best current theories held by the linguistic community.

This prompts us to suggest that the theory and practice of a language's speakers taken jointly is the broad context in comparison to which individual speakers' knowledge of meanings typically falls short. A narrow characterisation of an individual speaker's psychological state gives us a limited slice of biography and a partial grasp of the language. Given the finitary predicament any individual suffers, it is hardly surprising that his knowledge should fail to individuate meanings uniquely. But the same is not true of the postulated Explicit Speaker, he who knows everything there is to know about the meanings of the language's expressions.[16] A characterisation of those psychological states which constitute the ideal speaker's knowing the meaning of expressions would give us our best dictionary.

The trick in Putnam's thought experiment is that the people talking about water are ignorant, in the way people are apt to be, as to the best current theories about the stuff. So we who know something more about H_2O than, *ex hypothesi*, they do, can see

16 It goes without saying that we need an account of what 'the language' is. Here what is at least meant is: a relevant time-slice of that indeterminately boundaried phenomenon which 'the language' so loosely and misleadingly labels. But exploring this question is a major task for a much bigger format.

the point as to what else is needed for them to achieve successful reference: namely, to intend to refer to just *that* stuff, and not something that cannot be distinguished from it when one's level of knowledge about it is suitably impoverished. Putnam's thought experiment does its work because it premises that the speakers on earth and twin-earth should be identically ignorant in respect of what their referential intentions would be if they were ideally, or just more, knowledgeable.

Burge, as noted, spoke of 'the physical and social environment' playing its part in individuating meanings. The foregoing suggests that we drop the first disjunct. This is not out of prejudice against the physical world, but because appeal to it is unnecessary in explaining knowledge of meaning which respects individuation – that is, publicity – requirements. The point is to find the right sense in which, as it is surely correct to say, meanings are not in the head, that is, not solely determined by the psychological states, narrowly conceived, of individual speakers. The suggestion is that they are in our heads, collectively understood; that is, that meaning is the artefact of intersubjectively constituted conventions governing the use of sounds and marks to communicate, and therefore resides in the language itself. Everything we need to know about the meaning of expressions is to be found by looking at what we mean by them: this takes care of the intentional side of the apparent conflict; but what is meant by them is not a matter of my whim or yours: this takes care of meaning publicity and stability. It turns out that the apparently conflicting constraints are members of the same family, namely, those whose joint operations constitute meaning.

How surprising should a result be which says that facts about the physical environment of language-use are not essential to meaning? I submit: not very. For one thing, much of what we talk about, whatever ordinal attaches to the realm it occupies and in whatever way it occupies it, is not physical, and much of what is physical anyway does not constitute natural kinds. It is the view that nature divides itself up in certain determinate ways that makes us think we can miscall it, and that therefore what we mean is only partially of our own choosing. Opposed to the metaphysics of this view – how far it has to reduce to a version of essentialist realism is a matter for debate – is the kind of view

Quine, for one familiar example, takes, namely that the dividing is done by us and in our own interests, and since it is effected by name-calling, our intentions are in the driving-seat. Our purposes are thwarted, though, if we do not get a public and stable language as a result; so meanings have to be passed in committee. The broad setting for individual use is thus given by what we might describe as the community's intentions, in line with its theories.

If one wished for an entirely abstract move to make the point, we can note that an idealistic metaphysics is wholly consistent with our linguistic practice. If we wrongly think that water exists independently of our talking about it, drinking it, bathing in it, and so forth, but intend to refer to it nevertheless, then the correct answer to the question, what are you talking about? when one is talking about water, is 'water', and just as the OED has it. And this is because the meaning of 'water' is individuated by reference to what the correct use of the expression in the language consists in. What blocks a version of the twin-earth case, in which the ideal realm twins the material realm in the relevant way, is that speakers in the former really intend to be talking about what, if there were any, would be water; and if there is such stuff in the ideal world's material twin, that is what the ideal speakers would be talking about if it appeared in their world.

7

Explicit speaker theory

One thing we all agree is that meanings do not just fall out of the sky; they were and are at least in important part generated by what users of signs do with them. This suggests that the semantics of natural language is the product of the history of its pragmatics. It does not automatically follow, of course, that therefore the right way to go about giving a theory of meaning is in some sense to do it from the pragmatic end: but in the larger project I wish to suggest a reason for doing so, and I suggest that what increases the plausibility of this thought is evidence that certain problem cases in our understanding of language are amenable to an approach in which pragmatic considerations are given full emphasis.

I do this in this chapter by giving a brief sketch of part of a theory I call Explicit Speaker Theory, which, despite its grand name, is a modest attempt to provide a methodological perspective from which to comment on some familiar debates in the philosophy of language and mind. For present purposes, it is the simple and natural way that Explicit Speaker Theory deals with certain well-worn problems in these debates that prompts the suggestion that pragmatic considerations should be treated as irreducibly central to meaning.

At this juncture I should state that by 'pragmatics' I mean what, over and above what is standardly assigned to theories of structure, reference, sense and satisfaction conditions, relates to the use of expressions of the language on given occasions, where what the speaker intends to convey, and the means the speaker employs in conveying it on the occasion, are especially in focus. I want to say that among pragmatic considerations questions of force and point – for my purposes especially point – are central. These facets of linguistic behaviour include, *essentially*, considerations about interaction between speakers and their audiences.

I found, in working at these ideas, that they afford independent reason for agreeing with some of what Grice says. I can only claim *some* agreement, because Grice is professedly inclined to accept two things which Explicit Speaker Theory is not, namely, the distinctness of meaning and use, and the privileged role of a notion of truth in any account of natural discourse. Explicit Speaker Theory's commitment to arguing for the dominance of pragmatic considerations is allied to a view that notions of truth – which in my view is not one insubstantial thing but a number of different substantial things for which the expression 'truth' is a homophonic dummy – play roles of a different kind (I argue for this view in ch. 3 above). A major tension between Explicit Speaker Theory and Grice's theory is that because the former has it that the crux in meaning is point, which is to be explained in terms of speakers' intentions to mean something on an occasion, conventional meaning is to be characterised as the dry residue of speakers' meanings, agreed in the language community under constraints of publicity and stability (another view argued for here). Now Grice has given considerable attention to showing that speakers' intentions and conversational maxims are insufficient for a full account. Explicit Speaker Theory aims to suggest that from these resources a satisfying account of meaning can be brought into view without having to import considerations from outside the reach of pragmatics, suitably construed.

There are many debates about language which can be exploited to show how Explicit Speaker Theory pushes us in the indicated direction, but I will advert to just four very familiar examples, and a fifth less familiar one. The problem about using familiar examples is that the literature on them is large, so with no space to review it I have to be unceremonious; and also, everyone has a favourite view about these cases, so doubtless what follows will seem too swift. The cases are (1) the proper understanding of natural language analogues of logical constants, (2) presupposition-failures for certain uses of verbs of doing and trying, where the appropriateness of certain locutions comes into question because some implied condition for their appropriate utterance fails to obtain; (3) some questions about referential uses of definite descriptions, and (4) a certain application of the Twin Earth story. This looks like a heterogeneous collection, but I submit it as a virtue of EST that it identifies some patterns in the aetiology of problems arising in relation to them.

And finally (5) I suggest that Explicit Speaker Theory provides a way of approaching the question whether, for any given natural language, there is something that counts as 'the language', or whether a natural language is a vaguely bounded family of idiolects, perhaps as numerous as their speakers.

But first it is necessary to define an Explicit Speaker, and to explain why he is so called.

An Explicit Speaker of his language is one who so uses it that whenever he makes an assertion (and *mutatis mutandis* for other kinds of utterance) he:

(1) expresses his intended meaning as fully as, if not more fully than, his audience needs in the circumstances;

(2) expresses his intended meaning as exactly as, if not more exactly than, his audience, etc; and

(3) is as epistemically cautious as the circumstances do or might require, if not more so, with respect to the claims made or presupposed in or by what he says.

Together these conditions make the Explicit Speaker determining or overdetermining in respect of the point and epistemology of his utterances. Note that they do not cover the same ground as Grice's maxims – although there is some overlap – and they do not pretend to be regulative for ordinary communication. Together they make an Explicit Speaker of his language one who is in practice absolved a certain duty, namely, the responsible speaker's duty to stand ready to clarify, qualify or defend what he says if called upon to do so by hearers who have and are exercising anything recognisable as normal competence with the language in use. The Explicit Speaker is absolved the duty of restatement because he is by definition never in a position to have to fulfil it, as long as his audience is as specified.

The Explicit Speaker is of course an idealisation, and one which immediately prompts questions. So it is important to be clear about what kind of idealisation he is. Let us distinguish him from two other possible kinds of idealised speaker whom I shall call the Ideal Speaker and the Optimal Ordinary Speaker. (Strictly, it is only the former who is an idealisation, because there might in fact be Optimal Ordinary Speakers). The Ideal Speaker satisfies the first two conditions, but for a third has 'is omniscient'. Thus the Ideal Speaker is god or relevantly godlike. One immediate difference between an Ideal Speaker and an Explicit Speaker as I define the latter is that the language of an omniscient speaker would have to be apt for the expression of everything, whatever that means, whereas the language of a speaker who suffers the finitary predicament – is finite in knowledge and powers – cannot be guaranteed to be apt for the expression of everything. So not only does an Explicit Speaker differ from an Ideal Speaker in being subject to finitary constraints, but his language – which is an ordinary natural language after all – carries the mark of that finitude also. This might make it seem that the Explicit Speaker should not be so described, but rather that he should be thought of as an Optimal Ordinary Speaker, i.e. an ordinary speaker who simply is as careful and precise as he can be, and that is all. We might be trying to be such speakers when we do philosophy or law; so Optimal Ordinary Speakers – or 'optimal speaking' by ordinary speakers – might be relatively commonplace. But there are significant differences between Optimal Ordinary Speakers so considered, and the Explicit Speaker I require for my model. One is that an Optimal Ordinary Speaker, an ordinary speaker doing his best, must be allowed at times to be in states where the beliefs and intentions that determine the content of what he says are not transparent to himself. This means that an Optimal Ordinary Speaker may at times fail to satisfy (1) and (2), and at times all of (1) to (3). But by stipulation an Explicit Speaker is one who always satisfies all three. So his meaning, intentions and beliefs are transparent to himself. Another and consequent reason is that an Optimal Ordinary Speaker has the duty of restatement, i.e. he would fail to be doing his best if he did not stand ready to clarify or defend what he said if asked by linguistically competent hearers to do so. But his obligations here are a function of the defeasibility of his attempts to do his best as a speaker. By my definition an Explicit Speaker is one to whom this duty is inapplicable for the reasons given.

So an Explicit Speaker is better than (so to say) merely optimal; and he therefore comes between an Ideal Speaker and an Optimal Ordinary Speaker, although he is somewhat closer to the latter than the former. A second stab at a definition adds these comments to conditions (1) to (3).

It should be immediately added, if it is not already clear, that the Explicit Speaker is conceived as one whose interlocutors are always ordinarily competent speakers of the same language. He is not a citizen of a kingdom of Explicit Speakers.

Some comments are needed on the conditions. The third, that the Explicit Speaker is epistemically cautious in the way described, suggests that he is governed by an ethics of epistemic caution which at least imposes an obligation not just to be sensitive, but to articulate or to be ready to articulate sensitivity to the possibility of epistemic defeat of any claim presupposed or made on its occasion. This condition is vital to resolving certain problems, one of which I consider. But it is not a requirement that an Explicit Speaker should be regressively hedging about his claims, making explicit such protases to his remarks as 'if there is a world at all ...' and the like. An Explicit Speaker is not by stipulation absurd, only pedantic. But it is a corollary of this duty of – so to speak – maximal epistemic caution that the Explicit Speaker be as well-informed as is required to fulfil conditions (1) to (2). This is not a demand that the Explicit Speaker be an Ideal Speaker, i.e. omniscient: it is rather that his use of the expressions of the language should be conformable to what I shall later describe as a Best Dictionary for the Language – that is, one which makes use of the best current theories of what use of the language's expressions constitutes talk of.

A comment on the Explicit Speaker himself is prompted by the first two conditions and his correlative freedom from the duty of restatement, and this comment in turn underlines a substantial point often made about a feature of language. In line with (1) to (2), the Explicit Speaker never indulges in metaphor or irony if there is a risk of misunderstanding – which even with normally competent hearers there often enough is; and he never indulges in ambiguity. He is, in short, in danger of being a bore. But his potential boringness is interesting in this respect: that it reveals one of the constraints imposed on him by language (there are plenty of others). For whereas by (1) and (2) he shuns ambiguity, he cannot avoid vagueness, except by stipulative means, which he will not anyway normally wish to resort to. He is of course minimally vague: a major point of certain resources in the language, namely adjectives and adverbs, is the reduction of vagueness, allowing both ordinary speakers and an Explicit Speaker to be maximally specific; maximally but not completely, because vagueness is a built-in feature of language upon which a good deal of its utility turns. But this does not generate an inconsistency with condition (2), which is that the Explicit Speaker expresses exactly his intended meaning, for one can exactly mean to say what cannot be expressed otherwise than by use of a vague expression. For example: suppose the Explicit Speaker says, 'X is bald'. That can be exactly what he intends to convey, independently of questions about the degree to which X has less hair on his head than Y to whom the Explicit Speaker does not apply this predicate. It is of course possible for a non-arbitrary stipulation to be made with respect to some vague expression which precisifies it relative to a certain purpose. One can say that a person $n\%$ of whose scalp has a covering of fewer than n hairs per some measure, is bald. Suppose registered bald people by law have to wear a white hat on sunny days. Then the legal instrument which enacts this law would have to be precise: trichological police would need a definition to work to. Just such precisifications in fact obtain in registration of blind people to whom welfare benefits are due.

But as we see, an Explicit Speaker would normally neither need nor desire to go for precisification of vague expressions, however non-arbitrary relative to a purpose: for their vagueness is exactly what from time to time he needs. The constraint they impose is not a limitation.

These comments together give us a second stab at a definition of an Explicit Speaker which will suffice for the present. I shall sometimes speak of the three conditions as rules which bind the Explicit Speaker in his practice. Another important feature of Explicit Speaker-hood, a corollary of the third condition, emerges as the model is applied. I turn to that in a moment. First I will just mention what I take to be an informative contrast with Russell's attempt to describe a 'perfect language'. That was a programme aimed at specifying the underlying logical structure of natural language. In addition to the assumption that there is such a thing, there was a further, at least at the outset: that it admits of a uniquely correct representation. The ambition was to set out in algebraic description of logical form something which, like

Leibniz's longed-for universal characteristic, would completely and unambiguously represent what is said by any natural language. And this in turn was held to have exciting metaphysical potential, since the idea was that what there is can be read off from what the language says. Well: all I need say is that I propose we substitute idealisation of the speaker for idealisation of the language: instead of looking for the perfect language, let us try to describe an Explicit Speaker (a near-perfect speaker, so to say) of ordinary language and see where it takes us. I think such a task justifies the assumption upon which it rests, namely, that it is not the language that says things, but its speakers.

I turn now to apply Explicit Speaker Theory to cases. The suggestion is this: application of the theory reveals a certain pattern in what generates the problems, namely, a falling-short, either because of the usual vicissitudes of discourse in an imperfect world, or artificially by hypothesis, of an Explicit Speaker's conditions; and it therefore suggests a solution to them, which is to make explicit appeal to the point of utterance and/or to identify the epistemic deficit requiring remedy.

The first case I consider – and I consider all of them briefly – is that of the natural language analogues of the logical constants, classically interpreted. I assume familiarity with the standard examples, and just register them here. On a certain natural view, one central use of 'and' in English is to convey temporal succession, one central use of 'or' conveys the speaker's ignorance of the respective truth-values of the disjuncts, and one central use of conditional statements is to assert that accepting an antecedent is a ground for accepting its consequent, and normally that there is anyway uncertainty about whether the situation denoted or described by the antecedent obtains.

The difficulties felt about these natural uses of the natural language operators arise from their divergence from their formal analogues. Their content exceeds that of their formal analogues, and they are therefore more fruitful in implications. Suppose it is given that a particular disjunction is true. We thus know that at least one of the disjuncts is true. But we are not in a position to infer something of a different order, such as that an asserter of this disjunction is either ignorant of the disjuncts' truth-values, or might be dissembling, guessing, joking or some such. The additional content is provided by pragmatic considerations: those specified in terms of the speaker's intentions and certain contextual features.

Faced with questions about these divergences, our inclination is to look for mappings. Strawson, for example, held that the acceptability or truth of a conditional rests on whether acceptance of the antecedent is a ground for accepting the consequent, but that this is not sufficient for a conditional's truth or acceptability, for which the truth of the associated material conditional, entailed by the natural language conditional, is also required. From this it follows that whenever an associated material conditional is false, its associated natural language conditional is false also, and that there is a problem about what to say of natural language conditionals whose associated material conditionals are true but in which it is obviously the case that the antecedent states no ground for acceptance of the consequent, for some such reason as, say, sheer irrelevance of one to the other.

Explicit Speaker Theory offers the following extremely simple and direct way with the matter. For an Explicit Speaker, the governing question concerns the point of choosing to say things one way rather than another. Consider the conjunction and disjunction cases. Let us accept that the most natural construction to place on someone's saying 'he jumped into the swimming pool and put on his trunks' is that the circumstances were such that the man referred to put on his trunks in the water. And let us likewise accept that if someone says 'he's either in Austria or Switzerland' that the speaker does not know in which of the two countries he is to be found. In the first case, if the reverse temporal order were meant, the situation would have to be regarded as non-standard, or the speaker as not fully competent. Either way, the point of the utterance is at risk of being obscured. In the second case, if the natural implication is false, a different explanation of the speaker's point offers: the speaker dissembles, jokes, or something like. But both in the account to be given of the natural thing to say about what the speaker intends to convey, and in the account to be given of the ways things can go wrong or differently, the key is the point of the utterance. An Explicit Speaker by his rules seeks to convey exactly his point, and so if he chooses to say 'he jumped into the swimming pool and put on his trunks' rather than 'he put on his trunks and jumped into the swimming pool', or 'he put on his trunks while jumping into the swimming pool', or any other variation of the temporal relation between the jumping-in and putting-on events, then that is what he means to say. So an Explicit Speaker *means the standard implications* of saying something a certain way to be present in saying it that way.

The problems – or supposed problems, as this intuitive move suggests – of the divergence between the natural language and formal cases are on this view purely an artefact of taking too seriously the syntactic similarity of 'and' to ampersand, 'or' to vel, 'if_then_' to arrow. The meanings of the second in each pair are determined by their truth-tables, that is, by purely material considerations. But those of the first in each pair cannot be explained without reference to the pragmatic features which determine a speaker's choice of just this rather than that way of saying something: which is to say, his point. This is revealed simply enough by answers to the question, 'why would an Explicit Speaker say it that particular way?'

So the observation is that application of conditions (1) and (2) (the full and exact expression conditions) make choice of a way of saying something wholly deliberate, so that every natural construction to be placed on saying it that way is what saying it that way is intended to convey, so if – and we accept they do – natural language conjunctions, disjunctions and conditionals carry the implicatures identified, then if an Explicit Speaker did not mean them to be taken in what he says, he would say it otherwise. (He would, say, qualify appropriately.)

The obviousness of the point about *point* is easy to overlook. Choice of a way of conveying point turns on there being something that an utterer can rely upon in the way of an audience's beliefs about what the point of his utterance is, contingent upon the decribable facts of how the utterance is phrased. In the case of ordinary language 'and', 'or' and 'if-then' a definite set of relationships is entailed by context in the choice of those connectives. 'He jumped into the swimming pool and put on his trunks' *entails* that the temporal order of the events described is conveyed by the order in which the conjuncts are placed. So if we knew that our speaker were an Explicit Speaker, there could never be problem as to whether that indeed was the entailment about temporal order, or mere mimicry of the formal analogue of conjunction.

One should surely recognise all this as obvious. Stating it falls under Wittgenstein's injunction to assemble reminders, for its obviousness is helpful for the other cases, as follows.

The same analysis in terms of point reduces the problem in the second case I consider, namely that of what might be called condition-failure, although it turns out, as I shall claim, that this is a misnomer. The debate in Austin, Searle and Grice is as familiar as the foregoing, and needs as little setting up here as it did. The problem concerns what account should be given of what is implied by saying that – to take two familiar examples – someone omitted to do something or that someone tried to do something. Using those familiar examples from Grice, it is natural to take it that the sentence 'A omitted to turn on the light' implies that A might have been expected to do so, and 'A tried to turn on the light' that some difficulty afflicted A in this matter, and indeed, most likely, that he therefore failed to turn on the light. So it is natural to take as a condition of the appropriateness of saying 'A *omitted* to turn on the light', rather than saying he did not turn on the light, that in some way there was an obligation on him to do so which he did not fulfil, or that he had intended to do so but forgot, or chose not to, or the like. If none of these things are the case, then it is inappropriate to use the verb 'omit'. If therefore someone says that A omitted to turn on the light, an audience is thereby licensed to make the appropriate inference. *Mutatis mutandis* the same applies to the 'tried' case. Our inclination would be to put the point by saying that it is *a condition of the use* of 'omitted' and 'tried' in these cases *that the implications hold*.

The problem as standardly conceived relates to the truth-evaluation of sentences for which such conditions fail. Suppose it is false that there was an expectation that A would turn on the light, and A did not turn on the light. Then is one to say that the sentence 'A omitted to turn on the light' is false or truth-valueless? Well, consider the Explicit Speaker. According to his rules his choice of ways of saying what he does is governed by the requirement to make his point explicit. If it is standard to use 'omit' and 'try' in given cases because the point of doing so is given by these conditions for their appropriateness, then only if they obtain would the Explicit Speaker use them. This obstructs the alleged problem by stressing the directionality of the dependence: to use 'omit' or 'try' is to say that these conditions obtain. Here I shall restrict the notion of 'saying that' to: expressly conveys. ('Saying that' is not coterminous with *asserts* – for a liar 'says that' but does not assert – and we must be reasonable about what the utterer intends by way of implication of what he says: he does not consciously have to imply every implication of what he says, given that their number might be unmanageably large.) The point of an utterance using these locutions is not given by contraposing, although what the contrapositive says is true (that if not-X then not-A omitted): so in determining choice of expression an Explicit Speaker, as the speaker who is expressly mindful of what one is taken to be saying in saying something in this particular way, uses the expressions in question only if he means to say that the conditions obtain. To say that 'A omitted to do X' is to say that – giving this idiom full weight – there was an expectation that he would. If there is no such expectation, there is at best no point in using 'omit', and at worse it deceives the audience. For the Explicit Speaker, accordingly, the problem cannot arise. I take this to mean that there is no problem and that a moral offers: that the property of evaluation is not truth-value but 'appropriateness', understood as parasitic on point.

The third case is also a straightforward one for the theory: it shows that the appearance of a difference between two kinds of uses of definite descriptions is an artefact of an underlying problem-generator which the theory exposes. Recall the familiar examples: 'Her husband is kind to her', where the man is not her husband, and 'the man drinking champagne is happy tonight', where the man is drinking fizzy water. And we are familiar with Donnellan's view. Now consider the Explicit Speaker in these cases. He intends to say something about someone, and in the example cases what he wishes to say is that someone is kind to her or is happy tonight. In order to fulfil this intention he has to pick out the target of his remark for his audience. The possibility that a description which he believes applies to the referent might get the audience's attention to the target without in fact being true of it is one which falls within the range of epistemic defeats to which the Explicit Speaker is required by his rules to be sensitive and, where doing so is germane, to articulate sensitivity. So he means, and therefore might say, 'The man whom I take to be her husband', 'the man whom I take to be drinking champagne'. Now the descriptions refer by attributing something to the referent by means of which the audience can pick him out. In such practice all descriptions are thus attributive – they attribute to the referents they pick out a *property they are believed to have* on the basis of which they are successfully identifiable. For this latter purpose, it is sufficient that on the occasion of use there is a presumption shared by speaker and audience that the belief could be true. This is different from Searle's account, given in terms of aspects. Suppose, however improbably, that there are no other aspects which in the circumstances could direct the audience's attention to the man whom the speaker says is happy tonight. It would remain enough that it is a plausible belief for the speaker and audience to hold about him, and which the speaker can exploit for referential purposes, that he is drinking champagne.

It seems entirely natural to say that what the Explicit Speaker does in these cases is what all speakers are enthymematically doing anyway, as an entirely natural extrapolation of the cases shows: if the audience responds, 'he is not her husband, he is her lover', 'it is not champagne, it is Perrier water', the speaker replies, 'Oh well I thought he or it was such-and-such – but anyway you know what I mean'.

This does not defend in any way Russell's allegedly pure attributive theory, in which the form of the example is represented as 'the uniquest x to satisfy F, Gs', because the epistemic restraint built into specification of F imports something which is additional to the purely conventional aspect of the other expressions constituting F. We can best see what is at work by reminding ourselves of Kripke's suggestion. For Kripke, the distinction lies between semantic and speaker reference. For some idiolect, the semantic referent of an indexical-free designator is fixed by general intentions of speakers to pick out a given object by its means. Speakers' referents are given by specific intentions on specific occasions to refer to a given object. And again familiarly, Kripke identifies simple and complex cases; in the former, a speaker's specific intention just is his general intention. In the latter, his specific and general intentions diverge, but as a matter of fact he believes that his specific intention determines the same object as his general intention. He might be right or wrong but still succeed in referring. On this view, D's 'attributive' case is nothing but the simple case, his 'referential' case nothing but the complex case.

On the Explicit Speaker view, however, all cases are to be understood as complex cases. Reflecting on the oddity of Kripke's distinction suggests why they have to be so. It is surely never the case, intentions to deceive apart, that speakers believe that their specific and general referential intentions diverge. Their choice of designating expression is governed by a desire to succeed in making reference. So as a matter of fact speakers are always in Kripke's complex case: they believe that their specific and general intentions coincide. Indeed, the distinction between the intentions is not one that speakers make from inside their referring practice: it is one that retrospectively offers in theoretical reflection on the fact that many beliefs are defeasible.

But the Explicit Speaker builds recognition of this fact of life into his practice. So his is expressly the complex case: his specific intention to refer is effected by articulably cautious attribution of certain properties to the referent by means of expressions whose conventional meaning is apt for the task.

Among the points worth noting here are the following. A familiar contrast between conventional meaning and speaker meaning lies in the offing of those remarks: it is just such a Gricean distinction from which Kripke takes his start, but this way with the outcome hints that any account of conventional meaning is, *pace* Grice, parasitic upon an account of speaker meaning: that the former is, in a sense worth specifying, the dry residue of agreements forced among speakers seeking success for their intentions to mean. This is a point which lies just off-stage here.

The second is that what gave rise to the debate about a reference-attribute distinction is ellipsis: the thought is that making speakers express too little of what a model speaker – the Explicit Speaker – would say is exactly what generates the problem. And there is nothing philosophically problematic about ellipsis.

But now we need to bring in another feature of Explicit Speaker-hood, implied by the conditions but not so far exploited.

This feature comes out in the final case I consider: a certain employment of Putnam's Twin Earth argument.

Putnam challenged two received assumptions, the first being that to know the meaning of an expression is to be in a certain sort of psychological state, and the second being that the meaning of an expression determines its extension. These assumptions entail that psychological states determine the extension of terms. Putnam's twin-earth case purports to show that this cannot be so, giving us his celebrated conclusion that meanings are not in the head. Of course this applies just when the psychological states in question are narrow, that is, understood concordantly with 'methodological solipsism', the view that psychological states supervene on intrinsic states of an individual considered independently of anything besides, in particular without relation to environmental factors causing or being effected by those states. Now on Explicit Speaker theory the crux for meaning is point: explanation of what an utterance means has to make essential reference to what speakers intend to convey. This means that a psychological state privileged by the theory, *viz.* 'intending to mean p', determines the extensions of expressions used. Putnam's twin-earth considerations seem to block this. Do they? I suggest not. The claim I think we justify by appeal to Explicit Speaker theory is this – and here we introduce the additional feature of Explicit Speaker-hood required by the conditions: that 'intending to mean p' does indeed determine extension, under the two constraints (a) that the words used are used according to what I shall label 'the Best Dictionary', which reports the agreed, relatively stable senses of expressions employed as tokens of communicative exchange in the linguistic community, and which does so according to the best current theories of the linguistic community, and (b) that the Explicit Speaker's audience of normally competent ordinary speakers will so take it.

We get at this thought by noting something about how the twin-earth case is set up.

The first thing to note is an apparently tangential point, namely that rejection of methodological solipsism does not by itself entail some kind of realism about the domain of application of the terms whose meanings are to be understood broadly. For so far all that we have identified as required in addition to a speaker's knowledge of meaning is the existence of other speakers whose interactions with him and one another constrain that knowledge. If this is not enough to serve as the broad context, then we need to find the reason in Putnam's twin-earth argument. Does his argument show that unless there is H_2O and XYZ out there on earth and twin-earth respectively, Oscar and his twin could not respectively have meant 'water' and 'water'? That is not what Putnam sought to conclude: his argument was not aimed at giving a proof of the existence of the external world, but at showing that meanings cannot be narrowly individuated. So there are three assumptions at work in the twin earth case. The existence of the different waters – water H_2O and water XYZ – is assumed, as is the qualitative identity of the twins' narrow states, as in the twins' ignorance of current theories about water in their worlds. Thus equipped, the argument has no difficulty in arriving at its conclusion. But before we accept these premises in our acceptance of the conclusion, we should enquire whether the twin-earth tale could not be better told, because more economically and simply told, using just the idea that the meanings of expressions in a language are the agreed dry residue of speakers' meanings.

Any individual's problem is that he does not know everything that all other speakers communally know about the meaning of the expressions in their language. This is unsurprising: if some best and latest dictionary pooled a community's knowledge of meanings, it would be a rare individual whose linguistic knowledge came close. Such a dictionary would report the knowledge possessed by the completest speakers – Optimal Ordinary Speakers – including, for example, chemists and hydroengineers. Now let us bring in the Explicit Speaker, who knows everything in the best dictionary. Note that the Explicit Speaker is not omniscient, like the Ideal Speaker: he just knows the Best Dictionary, which is finite and fallible, but reports at their completest the linguistic community's dry residue agreements over what expressions can be used to do. In knowing the meaning of 'water' the Explicit Speaker therefore knows that, in the latest state of chemical theory on earth, it is stuff of molecular structure H_2O. And let us also introduce the twin-earth PS, who is by definition equally up to date. Then he knows that 'water' according to twin-earth chemistry is XYZ. In this idealised state of knowledge of meanings – that is, where An Explicit Speaker has at his disposal the linguistic community's best joint knowledge – we find that when he says 'water' he intends to refer to water, that is H_2O, or in the case of the twin-earth ES, then to water XYZ; and so in either case the ES's grasp of the expression's meaning determines its extension, and the psychological state in which his grasp of the meaning consists is broad. But this is not because it is related, causally or in some other way, to water, but rather to theories about water, because he is speaking in conformity with the Best Dictionary, that is, with the fullest shared knowledge of meanings, in accordance with the best current theories held by the linguistic community.

The trick in Putnam's thought experiment is that the people talking about water are ignorant, in the way people are apt to be, as to the best current theories about the stuff. So we who know something more about H_2O than, *ex hypothesi*, they do, can see the point as to what else is needed for them to achieve a successful reference: namely, to intend to refer to just that stuff, and not something that cannot be distinguished from it when one's level of knowledge about it is suitably impoverished. Putnam's thought experiment does its work because it premisses that the speakers on earth and twin-earth should be identically ignorant in respect of what their referential intentions would be if they were ideally, or just more, knowledgeable: that is, if they were, or at least approximated the status of, Explicit Speakers. Now the third condition in Explicit Speaker-hood was epistemic caution. The suggestion here is that it is a corollary of being epistemically cautious that one be as well informed as one can be for the purposes of satisfying (1)–(2). The Explicit Speaker, in obedience to (3), knows (or carries around and consults) the Best Dictionary. So when he refers, he does not do so under Putnamiam epistemic privation of the kind suited to making the twin-earth case plausible.

I conclude now by drawing a couple of morals. The point of the Explicit Speaker model is claimed to be that by applying it to cases like the ones just canvassed, we get perspicuous accounts of what is being said and done, and they show that the problematic character of the canvassed cases is an artefact of failing to give full weight to considerations made salient by the pragmatics of Explicit Speaking. What helps with the problem cases is appeal to considerations of point and epistemic aptness; the Explicit Speaker is 'perfect' in his practice with respect to both – and in being so is such that the problems do not arise for him. This, my inference is, suggests that we should look to beliefs and intentions for the basis of a general account of meaning.

In the first two cases the problems were generated by incomplete determination of point in the formulation adopted by a putative ordinary speaker. In the second two cases the problems were generated by epistemic underdetermination in the cases; the putative ordinary speakers failed in achieving their intended targets of utterance precisely because of it.

An Explicit Speaker perspective on the cases brings a salutary reminder to our attention. It is that no non-idly employed sentence of natural language exists outside a pragmatic frame. For every non-idle use of a sentence the particularities – how things are in respect of the utterer, his intentions, his audience, the current state of the language, and the circumstances of its use – determine the meaning of what is said on that occasion.

It is these two thoughts together that suggest the third – at this juncture I do not claim they do more – namely that the conventional meanings of expressions in natural language are the precipitates of the linguistic community's tacit agreements to place the use made of certain signs under publicity and (relative) stability constraints, so that the ends of communication can be realised. These agreements are the conventions which dictionaries report. Any account of meaning so understood would have on this view to make essential reference to the pragmatic considerations – and central among them, *point* – which figure thus in its genesis.

Now it is widely held that – and I quote Searle – 'meaning is more than a matter of intention, it is also a matter of convention', and in illustration he quotes Wittgenstein's remark in *Philosophical Investigations*, 'Say "it's cold here", and mean "it's warm here"'. There is no inconsistency between agreeing with this and accepting what the Explicit Speaker theory says is central. For one thing, conventional meanings are, so the theory seeks to suggest, the precipitate of intentions anyway: what an expression means is what , in effect, it is intended to mean by the linguistic community. For another, nothing in Explicit Speaker theory excludes the obvious, which is that the point of a speaker's

utterances, even an Explicit Speaker's utterances, cannot be individuated independently of facts about the conventional meanings
of the expressions he uses, the context, the speaker's attitudes,
and whatever other pragmatic features are required besides. But
what it does do is to say that point figures centrally.

By way of conclusion, and even more briefly than in the familiar
problem cases mentioned, I suggest that among the other things
Explicit Speaker theory can offer is a simple solution to the question whether there is such a thing as 'the language' for any natural
language. The thought that there is such a thing is held by some
to play the role that naive realism does in theories of perception;
it is the dumbo view, to be replaced by more sophisticated views
such as that there are as many paroles as speakers, and that what
we too loosely call communication is in fact a form of translation
or, more accurately, interpretation. A natural desire to respond
that at least a *notional* 'the language' is required to provide a
norm – which among other things can be invoked to explain such
phenomena as (say) the differing divergences of idiolects from
majority intelligibility – might be met with the riposte that such
norms are in fact constituted not by something which is genuinely
'the language' but by the family of idiolects of an historically
favoured class of speakers (the currently rich, the currently powerful, the people currently in charge of the culture. There could be
– after the revolution, say, there might be – quite different folk in
these roles, speaking a different family of idiolects). And so the
debate might proceed. But one thing that would help to give it
shape would be to offer something that could count as a criterion
of identity for 'the language' if there is such a thing. This is where
Explicit Speaker theory comes in: for such a criterion is offered
by saying: *the language* is what the Explicit Speaker speaks. And
this genuinely does offer a normative conception across which
mappings must fall if the very idea of an idiolect of some language is itself to make sense.

8

Understanding realism

It is by now a familiar claim that different things are meant by the term 'realism' depending on the subject-matter to hand, and whether it is questions about the truth of a theory that are under consideration, or, not unrelatedly but differently, questions about the existence of entities. I am not concerned with taxonomies here and so will go straight to the kind of realism I wish to discuss: so-called 'metaphysical realism' about the spatio-temporal world.[1] This realism is familiar because we all, in our non-philosophical moments at least, believe it.

Realism in this sense is to be characterised as an independence thesis, as follows: the world of physical objects and events exists, and has the character it has, independently of any thought, talk, knowledge or experience of it. This captures our belief that the relations in which thought or experience of the world consist are external relations: any difference they make to the world is inessential, and the world and its natural furniture could and would exist even if it had never been a relatum in such relations.

---

1 Dummett, M.A.E., 'Realism' in *Synthese* 52 (1982) pp. 56–57 (references to this paper henceforth 'RS'); *The Logical Basis of Metaphysics* (London, 1991) (henceforth 'LBM'), pp. 9–10, 325–326. Everything that can be said about the ultimately epistemological character of realism as Dummett conceives it can be said of Putnam's view of (therefore mislabelled) 'metaphysical realism' too; in Putnam's terminology, the property – 'Independence' – that captures the core of realistically-conceived truth is its freedom from epistemic constraints (*cf.* Frege's sharp distinction between truth and grounds for truth); the claim that truth is Independent is the claim that 'the world could be such that the theory we are most justified in accepting would not really be true ... rational acceptability is one thing, truth is another' ('Model Theory and the Factuality of Semantics' in George, A. (ed.) *Reflections on Chomsky* (Blackwell, 1989), p. 214). Any view that opposes this (any anti-realism) is *ipso facto* a thesis that truth (and our view of the world in general therefore) lies under the government of epistemic considerations. For economy's sake I restrict attention to Dummett here.

According to a certain kind of critic, the label '*metaphysical* realism' is, however, misleading. What is crucial to it is a commitment to the existence of given entities *independently of thought or experience*; so it is (says this kind of critic) fundamentally an epistemological thesis – more precisely still, it is the thesis that epistemic constraints are inessential to our formulation and employment of concepts of entities taken to exist in some domain.[2]

Putting matters in these terms suggests a distinctive take on opposition to realism thus understood, more familiarly denominated 'anti-realism'. Questions about the existence of entities in some class of entities turn out on this approach not to be at issue between realists and anti-realists about that class. Anti-realist theses are thus not defined by their denial of the *existence* of given entities; espousers of certain reductive theses do this, but they might do it because they are realist about entities in a specified reducing class (so reductionism is not defining of anti-realism). Rather, anti-realist theses are now defined by the claim that talk of what exists cannot intelligibly proceed without the support of talk about how we know what exists, the two discourses being internally related in this way: that the second is at least a large part of what confers sense on the first. Accordingly, what is crucially at issue between realists and anti-realists regarding a given class of entities is an epistemological question. The point is eloquently made – say defenders of this construal of anti-realism – by Peirce, writing on this occasion on behalf of the anti-realist party: 'But if it be asked whether some realities do not exist, which are entirely independent of thought; I would in turn ask, what is meant by such an expression and what can be meant by it. What idea can be attached to that of which there is no idea?'[3]

As implied by Peirce, the argument is that realism is incoherent because the content of our beliefs about the world cannot exceed the grounds we have for holding them; unless – and this is a crucially important rider – we understand the underdetermined aspects of our beliefs in strategic terms, that is, as recognisably serving as hypotheses or assumptions to which, as a matter of

---

2 Dummett, M. A. E., 'Realism' in *Truth and Other Enigmas* (London, 1978), p. 45. References to this paper henceforth 'RT'.
3 *Ibid.*, and RS p. 55, LBM, chap. 1, *passim*.

conceptual strategy, we commit ourselves as a means of organising our thinking about the world in fruitful ways. (This is not how critics of realism invariably put the point, and indeed it is the place of departure for a way of thinking about certain deep epistemological concerns that need not detain the argument here.[4]) Such strategic additions have to be made so that we can transcend the limitations imposed on us by our finitary predicament (our occupancy of parochial slots of space and time, with limited powers of perception, conception and reason at our disposal – even when our efforts are co-operatively pooled). But to be adequate to experience, and fruitful in their predictive and explanatory applications, such additions have to be controlled by experience, either by being extrapolated from it and thereafter lying under constraints of applicability to it, or, in the case of *a priori* principles, the latter alone. They are always defeasible if they are the former. If they are *a priori* principles of some kind then the conditions of their application to experience have to be, at least in large part, constitutive of them.[5] This can be expressed in terms of the conditions of sense for expressions introducing them, by saying that conditions for their use are at least in large part constitutive of their sense.

This states as neutrally as possible a point which could with equal propriety be borrowed by the critics of 'metaphysical' realism from the later Wittgenstein or from what Strawson calls 'Kant's Principle of Significance', which is that 'there can be no legitimate or even meaningful employment of ideas or concepts which does not relate them to empirical or experiential conditions of their application'.[6] On such a view, these expressions, accordingly, are not candidates for evaluation as true or false; they are to be instrumentally understood, as more or less useful in the tasks they perform.

The view that 'metaphysical' realism, characterised by the independence thesis, is incoherent, is a view which implies a distinctive positive thesis, which is that there is no account to be given

---

4 See Grayling, A.C., *Scepticism and the Possibility of Knowledge* (Continuum, forthcoming).

5 RS, *ibid*.

6 Strawson, P. F., *The Bounds of Sense* (London, 1965).

of the nature of a given stretch of reality which does not make essential reference to facts about thought or experience of it. This thought might, on analogy with the Principle of Significance, be dignified by the label 'the Principle of Anti-Realism'. It is a corollary of the Principle of Significance. It leaves open an array of more and less plausible ways of articulating what relation obtains between reality on the one hand and the conscious relatum, however precisely denominated, on the other. (So, idealisms – which are metaphysical theses, telling us what the world is made of – are not necessarily anti-realistic, that is, are not necessarily yoked to anti-realist epistemology.) Efforts to defend realism do not, therefore, fruitfully turn on refutations of particular styles of anti-realist theory, but have to show that the Principle of Anti-Realism itself is false. But this is the same as defending the intelligibility of the independence thesis central to realism. A defender of realism has to show, in other words, that it really is intelligible, as opposed merely to seeming to be so, that we can have what is sometimes called an 'absolute' or 'objective' conception of the world, that is, a conception of the world as existing, and as having the character it has, without any reference to knowledge or experience of it.

As implied at the outset, at least part of the problem that has given rise to this aggressive reconstrual by the anti-realist critic arises from a confusion in the very nature of the concept of realism itself. The confusion arises from thinking of given realms of entities in two different ways at once, or more precisely, from conflating two ways of thinking.

The first way is familiar enough in its various guises as a metaphysical commitment, typically to a notion of substance; but it is difficult to state precisely. It consists in thinking about the entities in a given realm as existing in their own right, independently of other things which cause or, more weakly, sustain them in being. Such entities might be conceived as having the status of something like Aristotle's primary being, or at any rate as substances conceived as those things (or that thing, for monists) which exist, and can only be understood as doing so, in some sense in and of themselves. This thesis has sometimes been called 'metaphysical realism'. I shall refer to it as thesis A. Some of the more heroic moments in the history of philosophy consist in efforts to clarify it, for what is at issue, after all, is no less than the metaphysics of being. But I am not confident that there is clarification ready to hand. The following hints at the difficulties.

Understandings of thesis A fall into at least two broad categories. Formulations like 'existence in its own right' and 'absolute and ultimate existence' suggest a full Aristotelian concept of primary *ousia*. This is existence which is basic to other, derivative, existence; it at least explains itself, and perhaps indeed – as in theological employments of the notion – it causes itself. It is not obvious, without further taxonomy, whether the latter, stronger, notion is coterminous with the notion of necessary being, but apologists at any rate standardly so construe it. A reason for caution is that giving a negative answer to the question: could there not be a conception of contingently self-caused beings, in the sense that other facts about the universe do not necessitate their existence? is not obviously called for by the terms of the question itself. For there might be nothing contradictory in a description of the universe, whether false or not, in which the existence of certain self-caused beings is denied; and the reverse would have to be true if the entities in question were to have a chance of being necessary in the required fashion. But no-one need go out on an ontological limb in this way to get a notion of 'existence in its own right'; there is always an epistemological limb to venture along, which says that it is just a brute fact, to be accepted as primitive, that there are certain things which exist in this primary way. To make it metaphysical *realism* which the thesis thus understood amounts to, a bruteness claim has to be taken as a candidate for literal truth. (The idea of explanatory self-sufficiency is an epistemic notion, note; which shows the close connection between these ideas, as a supposed explanation of epistemic independence, and that thesis itself as discussed below.)

Or thesis A might be taken more weakly to mean that, having been caused, a thing X exists as a genuine individual whose dependence on other things, for example food supplies if X is an animal, is only necessary in the sense of physical law, and hence is metaphysically contingent. It might be a fact that X is in this way dependent on things external to itself; but the point is that *any suitable* external will do, so there is nothing to which X's dependence is metaphysically annexed. Of course it could be argued that

X is dependent on a class or classes of things – say, foodstuffs – but this does not alter the descriptive adequacy of treating X as an individuable existent. Consider a pebble: in what sense can it be understood as a dependent individual once its causal history – its having been produced by cooling lava, say – has been discounted? In this guise the thesis aims at asserting the ontological irreducibility of X to its material and efficient causes, and the ontological definability of X in a scheme of things, with its own path through a world, say, or its own separately countable membership of it. This second aspect of the notion is a rich one, for it plays a part in a story whose other themes – individuation, identity, particularity – are familiar indeed. The idea of individual substances has its busiest employment precisely here. The connection between the two aspects is that asserting X's independence in this sense means that X is to be understood as not essentially or internally related to anything else, of which it must therefore be considered part or along with which it has therefore to be individuated. So it is a true individual.

The question of how, if at all, these two understandings of thesis A are related is a matter of controversy. One can hold some version of either without any entailment to versions of the other. The chief reason is that an ontology (a theory of what there is) can select a range of individuable, persisting and therefore reidentifiable particulars, whose status as such is entirely determined by their relation to a theory or point of view which finds it convenient to treat them as such, without concomitantly holding that these things are in any way ultimate. This is the case with the medium sized dry goods constituting the ontology of mundane experience. No-one I think would now claim that according them the status of basic particulars in our scheme (see Strawson, *Individuals*) means that they are the ultimately existing entities *simpliciter*. This would imply, for one thing, a new order of instrumentalism about physics. Given that the basic particulars of a scheme might well be epistemically but not ontically basic, and in acknowledgement of the difficulties attaching to getting to the latter from the former, some – even some contemporary (see the familiar pessimistic views of McGinn, Nagel) – philosophers hold that the veil of the former is impenetrable, and we are condemned to ignorance about how things really are.

There have, however, always been more optimistic metaphysicians, whose ambition is to identify what is or has to be basic in the sense of the first understanding of thesis A, and then to explain how whatever seems basic in the second understanding of A is connected to it – perhaps, at the neatest, by being smoothly reducible to it. The denotata of referring terms in folk psychology, for example, are for some (the Churchlands, for example) dummies, typically misleading ones, for referring terms in a future perfected science which will pick out something ultimate, deeper even than the physiological level at which attempts at explanation currently aim. (There are competing candidates: Leibniz's monads are an historical example. Only those persuaded that physics is metaphysics will think that fluctuations in the quantum field or superstrings – or whatever next – have that sort of ontological status.)

The serious difficulty with A is that there just does not seem to be a precise way of making the notion of 'ultimate existence' or 'existence in its own right' intelligible. It obscures rather than helps to speak, as we have seen, about ultimate things as *uncaused*, or *self-caused*, or *necessary*, or *primary*, or *basic*, or a *brute fact*. The argument of the metaphysicians is that because there is something, there must be something ultimate, in a sense of 'ultimate' vaguely connoted by the foregoing expressions; and they draw this conclusion because they feel that a 'ground' of being is needed for what there is, which either needs no ground itself or is its own ground. (Compare styles of cosmological argument, which employ notions of causality and contingency to just this end.) And anyway, talk of grounds keeps us firmly in the realm of metaphor. Another, allied, symptom of the problem is that efforts to give this family of notions content turn quickly into appeals to a different notion, namely, epistemological independence, discussed shortly. This is shown by ready allusions to 'explanatory' ultimacy, which at least often substitutes for the purely existential account being sought. But whereas questions of explanation mark out a logical space in a genuine problem, the metaphysical side of the ledger seems to stay blank.

As to the second understanding of thesis A, it seems a commonplace, and an unexceptionable one, that something must serve as the basic nodes of a scheme, to which reference can be made and by which its historico-geographic contours can be mapped; but as we see in the case of our dry goods world, such an ontology is determined by the schemers and their needs, and we live familiarly with any number of sometimes only partially commensurable such schemes, and their vocabularies, in our daily lives: for example, the perceptual scheme of medium sized dry goods, the explanatory schemes afforded by the biological and physical sciences, the folk-psychological scheme of inter-personal interpretation, and the sociological scheme of social explanation. It is a bold thesis which says that any one of these takes, or in a perfected state will take, reductions from any or all the others, or that all are smoothly saved, if we only knew how to recognise it, by a complete description of something else which is ontologically primary. The common sense belief, of course, is that the dry goods world imposes itself on us, rather than we on it, and our scheme carves it at its independently existing joints, because it has to: but we need only remind ourselves of Russell's remark, 'common sense gives rise to science, and science shows that common sense is false', to recognise that whatever A-type thesis we try to evolve from our epistemic needs, it had better not be precisely that one.

The second sense of 'independence', and the one which I argue is genuinely at issue in the 'realism-anti-realism' debate, is epis-temic independence. Someone applies such a notion if he holds that the entities in some realm exist independently of any thought, talk, knowledge or experience of them. Call this thesis B. Often B is expressed in terms of the 'mind-independence' of given entities. When those who discuss realism mistakenly contrast it with idealism, it is clear that they have mind-independence in mind as the chief characteristic of realism. This way of describing realism accords well, however, with more familiar statements of the position in terms of evidence-transcendent truth.

To make out my claim that B is what really matters in the real-ism debate, and at the same time to locate the issues with respect to more familiar ways of setting them out, I need to widen the scope of the discussion.

The question we are addressing is: what is the realism debate really about? According to the current orthodoxy prompted by Dummett, it is primarily about language, truth and logic, and much careful argument has gone into persuading us that if we think it is primarily about anything else we are misled. The claim is that what chiefly threatens to mislead us is failure to break free of traditional concern with questions about what exists. We should instead see the debate, the orthodoxy tells us, as an opposition between, on the one hand, the view that to understand a sentence is to grasp its truth conditions, where truth and falsity are understood as epistemically unconstrained properties of what we say or think, and on the other hand, the view that to understand a sentence is to grasp its assertion conditions. Much of the discussion about realism and anti-realism has accordingly focused on these issues.[7]

I agree that metaphysical issues are not primary, but neither it seems to me are semantic issues. In my view what is primary is the epistemological question of the relation between thought and language, on the one hand, and on the other hand the entities or realms of entities over which they range. To demonstrate this I shall use as a foil Dummett's thesis that realism turns on a commitment to a truth-conditional theory of meaning where truth is understood as evidence-transcendent.

Dummett began by thinking that commitment to the principle of bivalence is the hallmark of realism, and its rejection therefore as the hallmark of anti-realism. He later came to hold that bivalence is not sufficient for realism, although it is necessary; what is additionally required is acceptance of a semantic theory setting out the particular classically-based manner in which the statements in a given class are determined as true or false.[8] Rejection of bivalence remains, however, characteristic of anti-realism.

This change of emphasis results from what are now, thanks to the detailed debate, familiar points about why a rethinking of the connection between realism and bivalence is necessary, which show that commitment to recognition-transcendent truth does not entail commitment to bivalence, so that if for other reasons it proves desirable to abandon bivalence, a notion of recognition-transcendent truth nevertheless survives. One can be a realist, in short, whether or not one thinks that there are exactly the two

---

7 RS, *ibid.*
8 RS, p. 55.

jointly exhaustive truth-values 'true' and 'false'. Dummett's earlier equation of realism with acceptance of bivalence was motivated by the converse relationship, namely the apparent fact that bivalence entails recognition-transcendence; which, whether or not it is right, at least appears plausible. An implication of the detachability of bivalence and recognition-transcendence, however, is that one can have a view of the relation between the truth-values of sentences and the presence or absence of their asserters' capacities to determine what they are, which does not follow automatically from one's choice of semantic principle. This raises questions about the nature of the relationship as Dummett has it, for in his view choice of semantic principle *determines* the nature of the relationship between the truth-values of sentences and the capacities of language-users to identify them.

Dummett claimed to have noticed that what are often described as two quite different debates, the realism-nominalism and the realism-idealism controversies, in fact share a certain form;[9] and then to have noticed that they share this form with other debates also, for example those which concern the reality of the future and past, mathematical objects, and values.[10] The common feature seemed to be that a realist in any of these different subject areas is committed to bivalence. Dummett argues that to take this commitment as the mark of realism is 'preferable' to treating realism as an ontological thesis, in which the commitment is to the existence of entities of certain sorts, because some species of realism, for example those about the future or ethics, 'do not seem readily classifiable as doctrines about a realm of entities'.[11] On this ground Dummett concludes that '*in every case* we may regard a realistic view as consisting in a certain interpretation of statements in some class' (my emphasis).[12]

The interpretation in question is described by Dummett in terms of a classical two-valued semantic theory specifying how

---

9 *Ibid.*, p. 104. See also LBM, pp. 9, 345.
10 See Grayling, A. C., *Scepticism and the Possibility of Knowledge* (forthcoming), esp. chapter 2.
11 RS, *ibid.*, compare McDowell, J., 'Truth-Values, Bivalence and Verification' in Evans and McDowell, *op. cit.*, and Wright, C., 'Realism, Truth-Value Links, Other Minds and the Past' in *Ratio* XXII (1980), pp. 112 *et seq.*
12 RS, p. 55.

the semantic values of statements are determined by the values of their parts together with their arrangement. Any theory of meaning based on such a semantics will be a truth-conditional theory which is 'objectivist' about truth, that is, which is committed to a sharp distinction between questions about the truth of a statement and questions about anyone's having grounds for taking it to be true. This means that the plausibility of the semantic theory can be tested by assessing the plausibility of the theory of meaning based upon it. Again familiarly, it is Dummett's contention, as supported by, among other arguments, the 'challenges' over acquisition and manifestation of linguistic competence, that the objectivist-truth-conditional theory of meaning will not do.[13]

What is pivotal in this train of reasoning is that it identifies classical objectivist truth as the key to realism. But this, it seems to me, is a mistake. For the notion of truth in play crucially depends on a pair of prior commitments, one metaphysical and the other epistemological; it is these, and especially the latter, which really do the work in what Dummett describes as realism. And when one recognises this, one sees that Dummett has run together quite different issues as 'realisms'. His blanket definition arguably obscures rather than clarifies what is at stake in each of the different debates.

Dummett himself states that the realist conception of statements in some class turns on the idea that their truth-values are settled by knowledge-independent states of affairs. 'The very minimum that realism can be held to involve', he says, 'is that statements in the given class relate to some reality that exists independently of our knowledge of it, in such a way that that reality renders each statement in the class determinately true or false, again independently of whether we know, or are even able to discover, its truth-value.'[14] The immediate interest in this for Dummett is that such a commitment shows – leaving aside problems of vagueness – that the statements in question are bivalent, because they are selected as determinately true or false by an independent reality which settles the matter without reference to any cognising subject. And this is why he describes realism as a semantic thesis: it is 'a semantic thesis [because it is] a doctrine

---

13 *Ibid.*
14 RS, p. 55.

about the sort of thing that makes our statements true when they are true'. But he goes on to unpack the expression 'sort of thing' in a way which shows that its being a semantic thesis comes courtesy of something else: 'the fundamental thesis of realism, so regarded, is that we really do succeed in referring to external objects, existing independently of our knowledge of them, and that the statements we make about them are rendered true or false by an objective reality the constitution of which is, again, independent of our knowledge'.[15]

What this characterisation immediately shows is that the conception of truth at work cannot be understood otherwise than in terms of the logically antecedent metaphysical and epistemological theses which determine its content. The theses are simply stated. First, there is a determinately charactered reality. Secondly, truth-values are properties of statements which they possess as a result of standing in certain definite relations – the usual candidate is some sort of 'correspondence' – to that reality, the relations being external ones as required by the independence constraint; which is, thirdly, that both the reality and the truth-values of what is or could be said about it are independent of any knowledge of either. So the semantic theory (the theory of truth and reference) presupposes the existence of a determinately charactered reality (the metaphysical thesis) which is independent of our knowledge and confers, independently of our means or even our capacity for getting such knowledge, truth or falsity on whatever could be said about it (the epistemological thesis).

This epistemological thesis is in essence a negative one. It says that our conception of reality is in no way constrained by our capacities to know anything about it. More precisely, it says that the knowledge relation is external, contingent and limited; it states (a) that the objects of knowledge can and for the most part do transcend our powers of access to them, and (b) that the sense of remarks about the existence and character of these entities or realms is not governed by considerations relating to our epistemic powers. In the anti-realist view it is the incoherence of (b) which underlies the incoherence of realism, as we shall see later. Among

---

15 *Ibid.*

other things it makes realists construe (a) as saying that the independence of objects of knowledge from acts of awareness of them entails the independence of objects of knowledge from knowledge *tout court*. There is no such entailment: which is the starting point for a story to be told elsewhere.[16]

What is claimed or denied about the relevance of epistemic constraints is neutral with respect to finer-grained accounts of what those constraints are. At very least they embody a demand that whatever is required for a conception of some object of discourse, it should lie within the ability of discoursers to get it – with it being allowed that the results of epistemic co-operation, yielding resources which can be shared and distributed courtesy of language, count among discoursers' possessions. Given inherent limitations on individuals' powers of perception, reason and memory – a finitary predicament which imposes narrow boundaries even on what the community of discoursers can do co-operatively, as a whole – that demand is an austere one. It is what identifies our problem in the theory of knowledge: the problem of trying to understand belief-acquisition and justification, given our strategic need for beliefs whose content often exceeds the empirical grounds there can be for holding them.

The negative epistemic thesis has it that we can attribute possession of certain concepts to ourselves without having to provide, or even to possess, grounds for that attribution. It is natural to express this in terms of the meaning of the expressions we use in applying such concepts, not least because the most tractable – and often the only – way of specifying the content of a concept lies in inspecting what we say. But what a theory which takes this route turns on is the prior commitment to there being truth-conferring (and so: meaning-conferring) states of affairs whose existence and character is independent of our knowledge of them; which is why a realist holds that language understanding is not constrained by the terms of some epistemological story.

---

16 It is to Colin McGinn's credit that he has recognised this obligation and tried – heroically but unsuccessfully – to meet it; see McGinn, *The Subjective View*, for one attempt, and 'Can We Solve The Mind-Body Problem?' in *Mind* (1990) for another, premised on an abandonment of the first; and my respective replies in *Berkeley*, chapter 4, and ch. 9 below.

On Dummett's order of exposition, if one accepts a commitment to bivalence and knowledge-independence of truth-value, one is thereby committed to holding that there is a knowledge-independent reality which makes statements determinately true or false. In this way the thesis about truth and its semantic embedding appears to be the decisive factor. But the logical order of dependence among these commitments is, as the foregoing remarks suggest, the reverse of his order of exposition. The crucial commitment is to there being knowledge-independent states of affairs, for without this view already in place for the semantic thesis to presuppose it, that thesis is empty: we have no other way of characterising the concept of truth required.

If we adhere to Dummett's formulation, in which acceptance of bivalence and knowledge-independence of truth-value commits us to the existence of a knowledge-independent reality, we have indeed thereby identified what that acceptance entails as to its theoretical underpinning. But there is no converse entailment. It may be natural, but it is not obligatory, for someone to hold the metaphysical and epistemological doctrines in question, and also to hold the view about truth which Dummett says is the mark of realism. But it is open to someone to hold those metaphysical and epistemological doctrines and to make different moves over truth: for one example, to deny that truth is a property conferred on what we assert by the reality so conceived; or, for another, to deny bivalence. And someone might do this latter even if he accepted that truth is recognition-independent and is so because it is conferred by a knowledge-independent reality.[17] At the same time, it is clear that what a philosophical doctrine of realism seeks to preserve from our ordinary beliefs about the nature of reality is precisely what is conveyed by the metaphysical and epistemological theses which give natural but not inevitable rise to the view of truth in question. Given this, it is hard to resist the view that the metaphysics and especially epistemology of the matter are fundamental.

One explanation of the apparent pressure to think otherwise comes from the idea that any adequate conception of truth has to

---

17 RS, pp. 105 *et seq.*

rely on stipulative features. In particular, it might be held that a correspondence principle, for one of the two main senses of 'correspondence', functions regulatively in our account of truth, prompting commitments about the nature of the corresponding relata. At its roughest a correspondence theory of truth says that a proposition, statement or belief is true if it corresponds to 'the facts' or 'how things are', false otherwise. Three difficulties immediately present themselves: what is the correspondence relation? What are the linguistic or psychological entities which stand in the correspondence relation, whatever it is, to something else? And what is this something else, here vaguely denoted by 'the facts' or 'ways things are'? For all the superficial plausibility of the proposal that truth is correspondence between sayings (or beliefs) and facts, the debate it has generated has not yielded any satisfactory defence of it. Accordingly it has been suggested that in response to our need for a regulative conception of truth, we simply lay it down as a minimum feature of truth that it consist in a correspondence – leaving open the question of what in detail this is – between suitably characterised relata.

There might accordingly be a demand for an independence clause in a specification of truth – that is, one which asserts that 'the facts' exist, and have the character they have, independently of our investigations of them – precisely to serve our need to be able to mark off true beliefs and utterances from those which are not so. Given that it matters so much in practice whether what we say and believe is true, just that objectivist division is forced, and in the heat of the moment an utterance's failing to be true invites no closer scrutiny as to how it does: we do not stop to ask whether it fails to be true because it is false, or for some other reason (because, say, it is meaningless, or has some third truth-value, or is not a candidate for truth-value at all). The view that falsehood exhausts ways of failing to be true is doubtless a natural one to have arisen in the history of ordinary uses of language, a fact which might yield a moral for anyone inclined to believe that ordinary usage is sacrosanct.

But the need which prompts stipulations about the nature of truth is precisely an epistemic need (all practical needs are such, although the converse is not true). Viewed as a strategic commitment, a correspondence principle entails the allied but further strategic commitment to the independence of truth-conferring states-of-affairs from knowledge of them, because this objectivist attitude alone sustains what is required by the urgencies of practice – that is, exhaustive classification into 'true' and 'not-true'. Considerations of practice of course lead on to the drawing of distinctions among ways beliefs and utterances can fail to be true. But at the outset our view of the character of truth is determined by the controlling influence of our metaphysical and epistemological concerns, namely, those which constitute our commitment to there being a knowledge-independent realm of entities. The power of these concerns can be seen in the fact that they give rise to the very intuitions which are offended by counterfactual conditionals that appear not only incapable of determinate truth-value, on the grounds that there is nothing 'in virtue of which' they could be either true or false ('if God had created such-and-such beings, they would have done so-and-so' is a familiar example), but that they are not even capable of being either true or not true. Here the lack of something 'in virtue of which' an objective truth-value can be assigned suggests that there is nothing to be committed to antecedently which would sustain a notion of truth-value for the cases in question.

The tension in Dummett's account is not far to seek. His reason for characterising realism as a thesis about the truth of statements rather than as an ontological (still less an epistemological) thesis, is, as noted, that 'certain kinds of realism, for instance realism about the future or about ethics, do not seem readily classifiable as doctrines about a realm of entities'.[18] Yet he immediately goes on to define realism for any subject matter in expressly ontological and epistemological terms: 'The very minimum that realism can be held to involve is that the statements in the given class relate to some reality that exists independently of our knowledge of it'.[19] This is inconsistent, so one of these views must give way. It is not hard to say which. If the notion of truth which constitutes the Dummett hallmark of realism depends for its content on an antecedent commitment to there being an independently existing reality, and if, as already quoted, 'the fundamental thesis of

18 *Cf.* RS, pp. 68–69 *et seq.*
19 RS, p. 55.

realism ... is that we really do succeed in referring to external objects, existing independently of our knowledge of them', it follows that what we should say about those 'realisms' which are not readily classifiable in terms of entities is, simply, and on Dummett's own reasoning, that they are not realisms. Disputes concerning them are disputes of a different kind: and insofar as they raise questions about what concept of truth is applicable to them, that concept cannot involve considerations about the knowledge-independent existence of entities. And it is accordingly no longer clear whether the concept of truth at stake in these disputes is objectivist. When we find that a theory of meaning rests on a semantics to which that concept of truth is central, commitments of the metaphysical and epistemological kind at issue have therefore already been made.

One point, then, is that whatever else 'realism' might denote, it at least denotes a thesis about a realm of entities. This should hardly be surprising; even in traditional debates about universals and the external world this much is a common feature. But as we see it follows that if ethics and mathematics and talk of other times – especially the future – are not about realms of entities, then controversies over the concepts of truth and knowledge applicable to them are not realism-anti-realism controversies. On this conception, although we recognise that, in ethics, the debate is between cognitivists and those who disagree with them, and that in mathematics it is between espousers of different under-standings of what makes for the truth of mathematical state-ments, we also recognise that in neither debate is it just that there is no obligation to talk about the existence of entities (the respec-tive candidates might be 'moral properties' and 'structures'); it is, as Dummett himself suggests, positively misleading. For if, respectively, cognitivist and Platonist theses turn on claims about the existence of certain sorts of moral properties or mathematical structures, the question immediately arises as to how we can reduce the metaphorical character of such claims, given that their sense is imported from the one case (the 'external world' case) which alone has unmetaphorical content.[20] The absence of an answer to this question is precisely Dummett's motive for switch-

---

20 Compare Tennant, *Anti-Realism and Logic* (Oxford, 1987), p. 12.

ing attention to the problem of truth. But as shown, doing so brings too much under one label. The solution is not to find a different reason – one given in terms of truth – for classifying all these controversies together as realism controversies, but instead to recognise that they are controversies of severally different kinds. So we do well to restrict talk of realism to the case where controversy concerns unmetaphorical claims about the knowledge-independent existence of entities or realms of entities – namely, the 'external world' case – and employ more precise denominations for the different debates which arise in these other domains.

The most important point to be made about the nature of realism, however, is that what crucially differentiates it is the epistemological thesis that the realms or entities to which ontological commitment is made exist independently of knowledge of them. It is vital to note that existential commitment without this epistemological independence claim is not realism. For it is no-one's view that if the existence of something x can only be understood in terms of what it is for *x*'s existence to be known or detected, therefore x is unreal. Obviously enough, an anti-realist metaphysics is a metaphysics of existing entities. What differentiates such a view from a realist one is that unlike the realist, the anti-realist can make no sense of metaphysical claims without a supporting epistemology that yields grounds for them. If something is asserted to exist, in other words, it is because something counts as validating, supporting or making sense of that claim; in short, something counts as evidence for the claim, grasp of which plays its part in establishing the claim's sense. As a result an anti-realist takes the relations between existing things and the relevant kinds of epistemic access to them to be internal ones – from which it does not follow, as in some characterisations of anti-realism it is often taken to follow, that the existing things are 'dependent' (perhaps even causally dependent) on knowledge of them. This is a descendent of misunderstandings of Berkeley, whose denial of the existence of material substance is often interpreted as a denial of the existence of the external world.[21] Understood from this

---

21 This is why Berkeley is in no sense a phenomenalist; see *Berkeley, op. cit.*, pp. 95 *et seq.*

perspective, what is at stake between realists and anti-realists is the epistemological thesis that what exists does or can do so independently of any thought, talk, knowledge or experience of it. To substantiate his case the realist has to show that this claim is intelligible. The anti-realist thesis is that the realist's claim is unintelligible.[22]

Are we helped by recognising that the realism dispute is primarily an epistemological one? In giving an affirmative answer one must begin by stressing that ordinary discourse is, without question, realist in character. We assume that the entities we refer to exist independently of our cognising them, and we assume the same about the states of affairs which, we further assume, make true or false our assertions about them. Our realism at the level of ordinary thought and talk, the 'first order' level, is indeed rather promiscuous: we take literally a sense, to be informatively compared with the case of fictional discourse, of there being something we are talking about when we talk. Various ways of cashing this thought suggest themselves, one of which is that it would render explanation of our first order linguistic practice incoherent if we did not or could not attribute to speakers beliefs about the existence, independently of them, of the entities constituting the domain over which their discourse ranges.

The clue lies in the fact that these realist commitments are *commitments* and that they are fundamental to first order practice. We might now – to wax schematic – distinguish between realism, assumed at the first order, and what I shall for present purposes label 'Transcendentism', the second order thesis that realism is literally true. On this way of putting matters, anti-Transcendentism is the thesis that it is mistaken to claim that realism is literally true, since nothing can, on the realist view itself, establish that it is either true or false, for the content of realist claims exceeds the possibilities of verification of them. Rather, says the anti-Transcendentist, realism is a fundamental assumption of our practice at the first order. It is therefore not true but assumed to be true. The dispute between these positions is accordingly a

---

22 LBM, pp. 9, 319–320; Grayling, *Introduction to Philosophical Logic*, chaps 8 and 9 *passim*.

second-order controversy about the correct understanding of our practice and the logical and metaphysical presuppositions of it. Second order commentary might show that there is need to revise a first order practice wherever the commentary reveals the practice to be wrong. A second order thesis like this would constitute an error theory with respect to first order practice, as in the case, say, of Mackie's view about ethics.[23] But it depends on cases, for it can be that second order interpretation of first order practice leaves the latter as it is.

At first blush the difference between the Transcendentist and the anti-Transcendentist positions looks vanishingly small. But the consequences for a range of issues, including our understanding of truth and knowledge, are great. On the Transcendentist view the relations between speakers and what they speak about are external ones, so it is at very least natural to treat truth as a property which our utterances have conferred on them by knowledge-independent states-of-affairs, and our notion of knowledge as having it that whatever consequences, if any, our knowing something about the world has for the world, they are contingent ones only. In particular, coming to know things about the world is a process of discovery, one which lies under the austere constraint of our inherent epistemic limitations. (It is in this sense, to use Crispin Wright's phrase, that realism is 'modest'.) Taken together, these theses about truth and knowledge entail a commitment to there being a sharp distinction between a statement's truth-value and our having grounds for assigning it one. This epistemological commitment is sometimes identified by Dummett as fundamental to Frege's views and – quite rightly, as the argument here has it – as the crux of Transcendentism. For the anti-Transcendentist that distinction exists for us only at the first order, as a matter of epistemic strategy.

Either way, therefore, the nub of the matter at the second order concerns the question whether metaphysical commitments at the first order can be regarded as literally true (or false) as Transcendentism claims, or, as anti-Transcendentism claims, as having an

---

23 Here, in slightly different terminology, I reprise the point made in chap. 2 above.

irreducibly strategic character, constituting assumptions of our discourse which we hold true as a framework for organising experience fruitfully. It is a debate primarily about the role of epistemic constraints in understanding our thought, not a debate about what logical principles our practices should embody, nor a debate about what is taken to exist in our first-order scheme of things (or the science by which they are explained and, to the extent possible, manipulated). In this sense the debate leaves everything as it is, and therefore if anti-Transcendentism is correct, no revisions to logic, linguistic practice or mundane metaphysics are called for.

These ideas might be taken up and explored in more detail elsewhere. But before we leave the matter of identifying accurately what is at stake in the realism-anti-realism debate – or Transcendentist-anti-Transcendentist debate, as perhaps we should call it – we should keep the following in mind.

Earlier it was noted that current orthodoxy defines the debate as being primarily about meaning. But despite the fact that, if the foregoing discussion is right, the debate is correctly to be seen as one which primarily concerns thesis B, that is, epistemology, and one which moreover applies only where questions about the existence of entities are taken to be already settled, there is nevertheless no suggestion that semantic questions are irrelevant. Far from it. This is because a decision about the role of epistemic constraints one way or the other has immediate results for our view about what sort of theory of meaning we can have; and that in turn will tell us where to look for a detailed understanding of our concepts of truth, reference and the nature of valid inference.

Dummett is explicit in his opposition to this kind of approach. 'An attack from the top down tries to resolve the metaphysical problem first, and then to derive from the solution to it the correct model of meaning, and the appropriate notion of truth, for the sentences in dispute, and hence to deduce the logic we ought to accept as governing them.'[24] But the disadvantage of this approach, he says, is that we have no way of resolving the metaphysical dispute because, despite centuries of debate, we

---

24 WTM II, *ibid.*

cannot give it a clear content; we cannot reduce the metaphorical character of the terms in which it is posed. Therefore we should proceed bottom-up, starting with the question of the correct model of meaning for statements of the disputed class, 'ignoring', he says, 'the metaphysical problems at the outset'.[25] When the correct model of meaning has been devised the metaphysical problems will thereby be solved, because there is nothing more to a metaphysics than its being the 'picture of reality' that goes with a particular model of meaning.[26]

My response is to say, first, that metaphysical problems will only be statable in metaphorical or pictorial terms if we think they arise in connection with ethics, mathematics, the future, or similar subject-matters. One is much inclined to agree with Dummett that no real content can be attributed in such cases; or indeed in any case, for this is just the difficulty noted in connection with thesis A. But as argued above, this is precisely the reason for saying that disputes over these cases are not therefore realism disputes: they are not candidates for evaluation in terms of Transcendentist commitment, that is, commitment to the knowledge-independent existence of entities. The only subject-matter where this makes non-metaphorical sense is the external world case.

But in any event the top-down strategy does not start with the metaphysical problem, not even the unmetaphorical one: it starts with an epistemological one, namely, the question whether epistemic constraints are necessary for the intelligibility of our metaphysical claims and indeed for our discourse in general. Once that issue is resolved, *ipso facto* one rather than another basis for a choice of model of meaning has been laid. So much is implicit in Dummett's own characterisation of the notion of truth he identifies as the source of realism. The point here is to insist on the dependence of that notion on epistemological considerations, and therefore to urge a redistribution of emphasis in everything that follows.

---

25 *Ibid.*
26 *Ibid.*

9

On how not to be realistic

In the preceding chapter ('Understanding realism') I argued that: 'a defender of realism has to show that it really is intelligible, as opposed merely to seeming to be so, that we can have what is sometimes called an "absolute" or "objective" conception of the world, that is, a conception of the world as existing, and as having the character it has, without any reference to knowledge or experience of it.' Despite the vigour of the debate between realist and anti-realist perspectives in the assorted domains to which the dispute applies, there have been remarkably few full-frontal endeavours by those more sympathetic to the former line to set out the way in which an absolute conception can be arrived at from the finitary and local perspective of thought and experience on which anti-realist intuitions turn. Two of the most interesting and persuasive such attempts have been provided, in similar ways, by Thomas Nagel and Colin McGinn. They are eminently worth revisiting, as valuable contributions to understanding what is at stake in the debate. I consider two attempts by McGinn in this direction, the second of which entails abandonment of the first. McGinn's second attempt is close to considerations offered by Nagel, which I discuss in their turn.

McGinn's first suggestion occurs in *The Subjective View*,[1] where a major part of his concern is to argue that whereas perceptual experience involves irreducibly subjective elements reflecting the constitution of mind, this does not entail the inescapability of an anti-realist view, on the ground that an objective perspective is available to us by conceptual means.

McGinn summarises his view as follows: 'I suggested that perception of secondary qualities and indexical thought counted as

---

1 McGinn C., *The Subjective View* (Oxford, 1983).

subjective modes of representation, in contrast to the objective character of primary quality perception and non-indexical thought. These two exemplifications of the subjective view were claimed to exhibit certain quasi-logical laws governing the internal relations between the ways in which the world is subjectively represented: these laws have their source in the constitution of the subject. I also said that the identification of these subjective features enjoys a certain kind of incorrigibility, and that they operate as a sort of grid laid over the world by the representing mind. I then urged that these two kinds of representation are ineliminable from any mind capable of perceptual and direct access to the world.'[2]

McGinn's ground for these claims is his acceptance of what he variously calls 'the Berkeley point' or the 'inseparability thesis', namely that all perceptual experience is of both primary and secondary qualities, and that there can be no experience from which the latter are eliminated. This is, he says, a 'necessary truth about perception'. Because secondary quality experience contains ineliminably subjective aspects, and because secondary and primary qualities cannot be experienced apart, it follows that no story can be told about the way the world appears which can dispense with reference to perceivers of it. But because Berkeley took this to mean that no sense can be made of an 'absolute and objective conception of things', McGinn restricts the inseparability thesis to perception alone and claims that it does not apply to conception. 'My own view is that we should reject this inseparability thesis for conception but accept it for perception. To take this divided attitude is to commit oneself to a radical discontinuity between perception and conception: we cannot any longer regard conception as a "faint copy" of perception; it is not explicable in terms of an imagined perceptual point of view, indeed it is not strictly a point of view at all.'[3] Tying conception to perception in the way Berkeley does is one of the chief grounds substantiating idealism; detaching them, as McGinn says we should, leaves room for the claim that despite the ineliminably subjective character of experience, an 'absolute and objective' conception of the

---

2 *Ibid.*, p. 157.
3 *Ibid.*, pp. 80–81.

world remains available. He says, 'Resisting idealism ... requires us to reject the inseparability thesis for conception – on pain of making the mind-independent world literally inconceivable'.[4]

The first point required in response is that perception and conception are epistemic modalities, and that it takes a further step to make the quite different claim (as Berkeley does) that mental activity is causally responsible for the existence of the world of physical objects and events. This is a specifically metaphysical claim. McGinn is in good company in collapsing the epistemic and metaphysical in this way: the conflation is apparent, in the words just quoted, in the move from the metaphysical point about idealism as asserting the mind-dependence of the world to the epistemological point about the 'inconceivability' of the world independently of modalities of conceiving it: 'Resisting idealism ... requires us to reject the inseparability thesis for conception – on pain of making the mind-independent world literally inconceivable.'

But the point McGinn is making is after all clear enough: the resource for sustaining a realistic conception of a world independently of facts about how we relate epistemically to it lies, he says, in holding apart the two epistemic modalities in question; and this therefore is the crux of the issue. Can conception and perception be held apart as McGinn requires? The claim that holding them apart makes an absolute conception of the world possible demands that we specify a means of arriving at and applying concepts independently of experience, but which is such nevertheless that those concepts can be objectively descriptive of the world. How is this to be done?

McGinn says that he is not able to answer this crucial question. He dismisses two ways in which an objective conception could

---

4 *Ibid.*, p. 115. Note that McGinn makes the widespread mistake of conflating idealism and anti-realism; the foregoing remarks show that the former, as a metaphysical thesis, is to be distinguished from the latter, which is an epistemological thesis. The appropriate oppositions hold between idealism and materialism, which is a dispute about what the world is fundamentally made of, and between realism and anti-realism, which is a dispute about the relation of thought (experience, perception, reference) to things. For the purpose of the present paper McGinn's mistake – in making which he is in a large company – is not crucial. Chapters 2 and 8 above are at pains to establish this point.

be arrived at on the basis of sense experience but which prescinds from its subjective elements, one of which is a form of experience in which only the primary qualities are perceived, the other of which involves abstraction of primary qualities from the secondary qualities that always accompany them.[5] He rejects them for the reasons already given. And he then says, 'I do not have an alternative theory of how the concepts of the [absolute and objective conception] are come by', and suggests that a solution is to be looked for in the direction of the rationalists' idea of 'pure intellection', a 'means of mental representation which is non-sensory in character',[6] adding, 'it seems to me that a more rationalist epistemology is indicated ... the manufacture of concepts must be thought of as the province of more intellective faculties of mind'.[7]

These are merely gestures, and McGinn admits as much. What he says more about, instead, is the motive for having such a conception: 'we require a conception of the genuinely explanatory traits of an object ... we wish to have a unique and explanatory set of descriptions of objects ... we wish a conception of physical objects as existentially independent of us – a conception that permits us to say "if no perceivers had existed, physical objects still would (or could) have".'[8] And we have these requirements, he says, because 'to abandon the objective view is to abandon the idea of an observer-independent reality'.[9] In short, without a way of arriving at an objective conception we are left with an anti-realist viewpoint, and this McGinn is urgent to avoid. He therefore commits himself to the view that: 'Concepts suited to the objective conception are thus neither derived from, nor restricted in their application to, the contents of experience.'[10]

How plausible can this commitment be made to seem, given that it directly conflicts with the modest constraint on a concept's having content embodied in Strawson's 'Principle of Significance'? In this Kantian principle the motivating idea is that conception

---

5 *Ibid.*, pp. 124–125.
6 *Ibid.*, p. 111.
7 *Ibid.*, p. 126.
8 *Ibid.*, p. 115.
9 *Ibid.*, p. 127.
10 *Ibid.*

must be empirically anchored, because concepts apply to the world over which experience ranges, and therefore either or both their source and the conditions of their applicability have to be constrained by experience if it can legitimately be claimed that they thus apply. This, as noted, states a necessary condition of concept formation and application which distances what can count as ways of thinking and talking about aspects of the world from (for example) merely imagining. (Imagining is distinguished from conceiving, in the strict sense of forming and applying concepts, precisely in that what is imagined is free of those constraints.)

In the light of these points it is hard to see how to make a 'more rationalist' alternative intelligible. McGinn talks of concepts that (putatively) give us an objective description of the world, but whose source is explicitly *not* the world or our experience of it. Yet every consideration points in the contrary direction. The revisability of our world-applicable concepts in the face of experience shows how sensitive they are to it, a fact by now familiar from (among other things) the defeasibility of science. This marks the dependence in one direction. In the other, it is an equally familiar point that having experience just is to apply concepts apt for, because conditioned by success and failure in application to, the world. To have experience – as Kant went some way to teaching us, and *pace* Davidson on the 'third dogma' – is to order, interpret, and organise input on the basis of a scheme of concepts whose possession by us is tailored to the task.

Considerations about the dependence in the first direction are enough to show why rationalism, in McGinn's sense, fails. The deliverances of reason unconstrained by empirical tests cannot be distinguished from consistent fairy tales, and nothing beyond a *merely* internal standard of coherence for any theory thus constructed can give reason for accepting it as true – especially since on this view it is not truth to or of the world as it is encountered in experience which can be at issue, for then the concepts deployed would be attached to empirical conditions of derivation and application, which is expressly ruled out.

Nor, further, are we helped by McGinn's invoking the notion of an 'intellective faculty' which gives us, independently of experience, a grasp of the nature of the world as it is in itself; for what such a faculty can be, and how it grasps the essence of the world, is by McGinn's own admission unclear. Rationalists tempted by the view that knowledge of what the world is like in its true and ultimate nature – putatively obscured by the way it appears – rely less, on the whole, on a claim that we have a capacity for directly intuiting the metaphysical facts, than on one or another of two broad but not exclusive alternatives. One is the claim that excogitation from self-evident or self-justifying first principles will lead to a grasp of what the universe must be like (taking the modality seriously). The other is innatism. These positions are not exclusive because one could, on this family of views, deduce – and thus in effect remember – what one innately but immemoriously knows.

No doubt these options for a rationalist epistemology are not exhaustive, but it demands ingenuity to devise others less implausible than they. What McGinn means, therefore, by 'pure intellection ... a means of representation which is non-sensory in character' is obscure.[11] One can make sense of pure intellection in the case, say, of certain mathematical structures, for example in topology, where what is described does not admit of being grasped except through its formal properties. A Kline bottle in four-dimensional space is such a thing. But the manipulation of formal structures in this sense is not a perceptual representation or, if it describes what can be encountered in experience – knots, a Mobius strip, Euler's bridges – there is a straightforward sense in which experience gives content to their being such representations, an understanding not securable by other means. This again illustrates the difficulty with McGinn's suggestion: if the absolute conception of the world is, as he puts it, 'radically discontinuous' with experience of the world, what substantiates the claim that it is a conception of the world? This repeats, from another direction, the fairy-tale charge.

Some of what McGinn says about the ineliminability of subjectivity from experience has an avowedly Kantian flavour.[12] He does not however subscribe to Kant's chief claim, which is that objectivity is the result of the application of *a priori* concepts in experience, since this would, in the end, amount to denying that we can

---

11 *Ibid.*, p. 111.
12 *Ibid.*, pp. 106, 157.

give content to an absolute conception, for the two reasons that in Kant's view those concepts are, first, constitutional aspects of the forms of sensibility (space and time) and the understanding (the categories), and hence are subjective in McGinn's sense, that is, are supplied by the mind; and secondly, are 'empty' unless they lie under empirical conditions of applicability. On neither count therefore can Kant's view satisfy McGinn, which is no doubt why he does not comment on it. But in the absence of some such resource for explaining how we can possess *a priori* the concepts that make for an objective conception, given the inadequacy of the rationalist alternative, it is not clear where else to look. This means there is no sustainable way of allowing an inseparability thesis for perception while rejecting it for conception, and that consequently there is no way of attaching sense to talk of 'an absolute and objective conception of the world' by this means.

McGinn's attempt, as described in the foregoing, is to provide what Nagel calls 'objective transcendence', a no-point-of-view viewpoint from which to give an account of how things are.[13] His second attempt retains this aim, but is tacitly premised on an abandonment of the first attempt. The first turns on reviving rationalist epistemology; the second turns on abandoning epistemology altogether. It consists in saying that we are constitutionally incapable of escaping our ignorance about regions of reality which transcend our cognitive capacities. The argument occurs in connexion with a discussion of whether the mind-body problem is solvable,[14] but it is intended to have more general application, because at the end of his discussion McGinn argues that 'the limits of our minds are ... not the limits of reality. It is deplorably anthropocentric to insist that reality be constrained by what the human mind can conceive'.[15] So when regions of reality 'systematically elude our cognitive grasp' this is no reason for taking it that attempts to think about these unthinkable regions of reality are nonsensical.[16] And this McGinn takes to afford us a 'vision

---

13 Nagel, T., *Mortal Questions* (Cambridge, 1979), p. 209; *The View From Nowhere* (Oxford, 1986), *passim* .
14 McGinn, C., 'Can We Solve The Mind-Body Problem?' in *Mind*, 1989.
15 *Ibid.*, p. 366.
16 *Ibid.*, p. 365.

of reality (a metaphysics) that makes it truly independent of our given cognitive powers'.[17]

The argument to this conclusion turns on the notion of 'cognitive closure'. It proceeds as follows. A type of mind is cognitively closed with respect to something x if and only if the concept-forming procedures available to that type of mind cannot give it a grasp of x. Minds come in different kinds; what some can grasp others cannot. For example, monkeys can conceive of things that rats cannot, and humans can conceive of things monkeys cannot.[18] A good example of closure is afforded by the perceptual case: some creatures can perceive things – certain ranges of the electromagnetic spectrum – which others cannot. This is simply a function of the way different creatures are constituted. 'But such closure does not reflect adversely on the reality of the properties that lie outside the representational capacities in question; a property is no less real for not being reachable from a certain kind of perceiving and conceiving mind. The invisible parts of the electromagnetic spectrum are just as real as the visible parts, and whether a specific kind of creature can form conceptual representations of these imperceptible parts does not determine whether they exist. Thus cognitive closure with respect to P does not imply irrealism about P. That P is (as we might say) noumenal for M does not show that P does not occur in some naturalistic scientific theory T – it shows only that T is not cognitively accessible to M. Presumably monkey minds and the property of being an electron illustrate this possibility. And the question must arise as to whether human minds are closed with respect to certain true explanatory theories. Nothing, at least, in the concept of reality shows that everything real is open to the human concept-forming faculty – if, that is, we are realists about reality.'[19]

Two different arguments, neither of them successful, and one important equivocation, are at work at the same time in this: an argument by extrapolation, an equivocation over inference to unobservables and supposed grasp of the cognitively inaccessible

---

17 *Ibid.*

18 *Ibid.*, p. 350.

19 *Ibid.*, p. 351. The last remark begs the question, but I ignore it in order to address what can be offered as McGinn's best case.

(an equivocation made possible by sliding from the case of perceptual closure to that of cognitive closure), and an argument from ignorance. I take each in turn.

All these considerations are directed against the anti-realist point that if supposed items or regions of reality are cognitively inaccessible to us, claims about their existence and character lack content. McGinn's argument is that cognitive closure considerations legitimate realism about inaccessibles because in effect they give us a handle on how we can think there can be such things – on how, indeed, we can conceive of the inconceivable, which is what, of course, the conceptually inaccessible is. On one of the arguments this is done by saying: monkeys can think things that rats cannot, dogs can hear things that humans cannot, therefore there can be things not merely which have, contingently, not been sensed or thought, but which cannot be sensed or thought by some of the minds in question. Therefore there can be things which cannot be sensed or thought by us. Then McGinn says: since there are inaccessibles from the point of view of minds less well placed than our own, we are entitled to go further than merely to claim that there can be things inaccessible to us; it is not just that there *can be*, it is that *there are*, things inaccessible to us – as witness the fact that the solution to the mind-body problem is made intelligible by these thoughts, for they license the conjunction of these claims: '(i) there exists some property of the brain that accounts naturalistically for consciousness; (ii) we are cognitively closed with respect to that property.'[20]

This is the argument by extrapolation. In Chapter 1 of McGinn's story, humans know things monkeys cannot know; in Chapter 2 there are things humans cannot know; and the intelligibility of Chapter 2 is supposed to rest on that of Chapter 1. But clearly Chapter 2 does not follow from Chapter 1, nor is it made more persuasive by it. A weaker argument, in which Chapter 2 has it that there could be things humans cannot know, at first glance looks more plausible, and is the most that McGinn should be trying to substantiate. But it does not work either. To tease out the problem here note first the modality in play. The two-chapter

---

20 *Ibid.*, pp. 351–352.

argument is not about what monkeys and humans contingently do not know – it does not concern what might yet be found out, say – but about what they cannot know. Secondly, note that the argument offers itself as turning on the principle *ab esse ad posse*, from *what is* to *what is possible*. This principle permits the following inference: it is the case that we know things monkeys cannot. Therefore it is possible that certain creatures cannot know things that can be known by other creatures. On this basis it is suggested in Chapter 2 that it makes sense to say that there could be things that cannot be known by creatures like us. Call this story A. As we have seen, McGinn tries to infer something both different and stronger: from the fact that we know things monkeys cannot, he infers that there are things we not only do not but cannot know.[21] Call this Story B. In it he does not merely infer that it is possible for there to be things that we cannot know, as Story A has it; he infers that there are actually things we cannot know. And this indeed is what metaphysical realism focally consists in: an existential claim about what transcends our cognitive capacities and for a belief in whose existence we therefore have no grounds.

The point about the two-chapter story is, as noted, that we think we make sense of Chapter 2 on the basis of Chapter 1. To see why the move is illegitimate, consider Story A. If this weaker and therefore more plausible version fails, so *a fortiori* does McGinn's preferred Story B. Story A makes covert use of the fact that if a comparison between the Chapter 2 situation and the Chapter 1 situation is to hold, there must from the Chapter 2 viewpoint be available a conception of better-placed epistemic agency for which what is unknowable to the Chapter 2-ers (ourselves) is or can be known. This is because the idea in Chapter 1 of something unknowable to certain kinds of minds is a *relative* notion: the unknowability is not intrinsic to the object, but is conferred by the incapacity of the minds in question; and therefore the unknowability neither is nor can be total, because the notion of something unknown and unknowable *tout court* is the notion of something

---

21 There is a short way with this. It is to ask: how do we know? The point is that Chapter 1, about monkeys, does not give us this knowledge; it only gives us knowledge about the disparity which as a matter of fact obtains between monkeys and humans.

empty. ('There is something about which nothing whatever can be known by any knower whatever': here words are idling.) Therefore, sense can be made of the idea that something can be unknowable with respect to given minds only if it is knowable to better equipped or better placed minds. So in Story A the Chapter 2 situation is covertly made intelligible by the notion of possible mind or minds which stand in relation to us as we stand to monkeys in Chapter 1. In Chapter 1 we can be confident that there are things monkeys cannot know because those things are known by humans. What provides the basis for comparison in Chapter 2? The notion of comparably superior epistemic agency for the Chapter 2 situation might be given content by (say) theistic views; otherwise it is science fiction; in any case it represents too heavy a price to pay for the intelligibility of the two chapter story.[22] For the grounds we have for asserting the possibility of there being such mind or minds – a notion of epistemic agency better placed than ourselves – is, since such agency counts among the inaccessibles from our point of view, as bad as those we have for asserting the existence of any other kind of inaccessible. So defending our commitment to the existence of the latter by invoking the existence of such agency is either circular, or involves an infinite regress of better and better placed epistemic agencies in chapters of higher ordinality. Either way the strategy fails: Story A does not make it plausible that there could be things (or truths) we cannot know.

The equivocation in McGinn's account involves a slide from the perceptual to the cognitive case. Perceptual closure consists in the constitutional inability of members of one species to perceive things which members of another, differently endowed, species can. No creatures are able to perceive all the properties of a given thing. So a property is not unreal simply because it is perceptually inaccessible to members of a given species. 'The invisible parts of the electromagnetic spectrum are just as real as the visible parts,' McGinn points out, 'and whether a specific kind of creature can form conceptual representations of these imperceptible parts does not determine whether they exist. Thus cognitive closure with

---

22 Note Dummett's Principle K in connection with this; 'What is a Theory of Meaning? II' in Evans, G., and McDowell, J., *Truth and Meaning* (Oxford, 1975).

respect to P does not imply irrealism about P.'[23] McGinn moves
from the fact that there can be perceptual closure on the part of
certain creatures with respect to a property which is not perceptually closed to other creatures, to the claim that cognitive closure
does not imply irrealism. Once again this is a two-chapter story,
a slightly different one. In Chapter 1 different creatures perceive
different aspects of the world. These different aspects are no less
real for being inaccessible to one or some of the creatures there.
This is explained by the fact that they are not perceptually inaccessible to others of the creatures there. In Chapter 2 supposed
aspects of the world *cognitively* closed to us are asserted to exist.

The leap from Chapter 1 to Chapter 2 is too obviously large to
invite much comment. It is not just that the Chapter 1 considerations do not entail the claim in Chapter 2; it is that they do not
succeed in the weaker heuristic task of rendering them more plausible. Note that in Chapter 2 it is not that we fail to perceive
something that other creatures do; nor even that we fail to conceive what other creatures are supposed to (although the question
arises: how would we know that they do, since what they putatively conceive we *ex hypothesi* cannot?). Rather, we are talking
about something, unknown and unknowable to us, which we
assert to exist on the grounds that, in Chapter 1, some creatures
perceive what others cannot. But no connection has been established here, and the contingencies of differing perceptual capacities do nothing to explain how considerations about cognitive
closure succeed in supporting realism.

It is true that perceptual closure does not entail cognitive closure, not just because of the contingent facts noted above but
because inference to unobservables from observables, together
with an understanding of their properties, is a legitimate and
indeed necessary part of making sense of perceptual experience.
But McGinn thinks that it follows from this innocuous truth that
cognitive closure does not entail irrealism about unthinkable entities. He seems to take it that since regions of reality perceptually
closed to a given creature can nevertheless be inferred by that
creature from what is perceptually open to it, the same can be
said in the conceptual case. Again, the difficulty hardly needs

---

23 McGinn, *op. cit.*, p. 351.

stating: it is that if we are serious in describing the properties, entities, or whatever they are, as cognitively inaccessible (unthinkable, unknowable), then there cannot be inference to them – for inference is a form of cognitive access and this is ruled out *ex hypothesi*. So from facts about different contingent perceptual powers and their limitations among different creatures – all of which is unexceptionable – we cannot hope to make intelligible the claim that we can conceive of the existence of inconceivable (not merely unperceivable, still less contingently unperceived or not yet perceived) things.

We take it that conceiving of the existence of unperceivable things is straightforward: we do it by inference, or we perceive effects of the unobservables, and both (related) forms of access are standard in the natural sciences. It might be left open whether such forms of access constitute indirect perception, and leave aside cases where the inference to, or indirect perception of, something relates specifically to that something being contingently unperceived (because we do not yet have the instruments required, etc.) in order to obviate difficulties about the implication of taking the modality in 'unperceivable' seriously. For McGinn's case to go through, it is required that we can make sense of an existential claim relating to something to which we have no cognitive access, indirect or otherwise.

Both the extrapolation story and the attempt to draw parallels between the perceptual and conceptual cases are efforts to block an entailment from inconceivability to irrealism. But there is another and more direct argument in McGinn's account, which might be called an 'argument from ignorance'. It is suggested by an analogy McGinn himself draws with theological perplexity about the properties of a deity.[24] Suppose we find that a notion of a god who is omnipotent and wholly benevolent is inconsistent with the presence in the world of moral and especially natural evil; or that the notion of omnipotence is inconsistent with the thought that not even a god can do what is logically impossible; and so on. A recourse for the faithful is to say not that these considerations render unintelligible the notion of a deity, but that our

24 *Ibid.*, p. 354.

ignorance incapacitates us for seeing, from the deity's viewpoint, how there just are no such problems. The usual way of expressing this is to say that our finite minds cannot comprehend an infinite being. One therefore solves the problem by drawing the veil of our own ignorance over them. (This reminds one of Descartes' last solution to the mind-body problem: that it is best solved by being ignored.) And of course this is a very useful and time-saving manoeuvre. For the purpose of defending realism, one does not say that if something cannot be conceived one cannot therefore have grounds to assert its existence, but instead that its inconceivability is not a problem with it but with us, is a function of our ignorance; and therefore its existence can be asserted. A little rephrased, the claim is: it is not that *there are no grounds* for asserting the existence of something inconceivable, but that *we have no grounds* for asserting its existence, and this latter does not entail its non-existence.

This makes clear, from a different direction, a familiar point about what is central to realist arguments. For the realist, there is one sense in which metaphysical and epistemological questions have to be held strictly apart. Questions about what there is must be treated as having nothing to do with questions about how we know what there is. This means that it is crucial to the realist case, as McGinn's arguments show, that to say that something x is not cognitively accessible to us is not the same as saying that thought or talk of x makes no sense to us. The anti-realist insists on the reverse; his position is that cognitive access to x (of which perceiving is one example) is a condition of understanding discourse about x. For McGinn and realists generally, having no means of gaining cognitive access to something is no bar to the intelligibility of asserting its existence. The anti-realist criticism of this is that in the absence of means to conceive of or to come to know about some putative thing, one has no grounds either for asserting or denying its existence; indeed they are puzzled as to how realists tell which we are to do.

Arguments from cognitive closure and ignorance are a far cry from a 'new rationalist epistemology'. They represent, as noted, an abandonment of epistemology. It is not surprising that McGinn should come to this expedient, for it is the logical terminus of holding epistemological and metaphysical questions strictly apart.

As we see, realists have to do this because the epistemological considerations always promise to influence metaphysical considerations in ways uncongenial to them. McGinn's first effort – the idea of a new rationalism – was an attempt to provide an epistemology sanitary for realism. His later arguments give up the epistemological battle altogether; we do not have to fight it if we can be realists under 'cognitive closure'. The new rationalist epistemology was still a form of cognitivism; the idea of there being wholesale blanks in our cognitive capacities, behind which reality noumenally – transcendently – lurks, is non-cognitivism. So McGinn's later non-cognitivist arguments repudiate his earlier attempt at an empirically unconstrained cognitivist position. But evasion of the epistemological issue is precisely what the anti-realist resists, for abandonment of any attempt to substantiate claims about the knowledge-transcendent existence of given entities means that we can say what we like: we can assert or with equal propriety deny that the fundamental reality is – take your pick – say, chocolate mousse. Bare assertion, charges the anti-realist, replaces principled defence of existential commitments.

There are strong similarities between McGinn's later views and those of Nagel. Nagel's account of the distinction between subjectivity and objectivity is familiar. He regards them as relative notions, constituting a polarity. The essence of the objective viewpoint is 'externality or detachment', a view from nowhere.[25] 'We flee the subjective,' he writes, 'under the pressure of an assumption that everything must be something not to any point of view, but in itself'.[26] Pursuing the objective involves self-transcendence in two ways, token and type: transcendence of one's own particularity, and of the point of view of one's species. The enterprise assumes that what is represented in experience or thought 'is detachable from the mode of representation'.[27] But the enterprise involves difficulty, for there are irreducibly subjective perspectives which more objective viewpoints cannot accommodate, 'indigestible lumps' such as selfhood, consciousness, freedom, and secondary

---

25 Nagel, *Mortal Questions*, p. 208.
26 *Ibid.*
27 *Ibid.*, p. 209.

quality perception.[28] So the 'only solution', in Nagel's view, 'is to resist the voracity of the objective appetite', and to accept that both pictures are incomplete.[29] This means that we have to live with the idea that 'there is no single way things are in themselves', that there is 'no single world'.[30] Whether this implies relativism, or is to be understood literally to mean that reality is intrinsically multiple or indeterminate in character, Nagel does not explain.

But despite concluding that 'objectivity has its limits' Nagel by no means takes this to imply, as one might expect, a rejection of realism.[31] One might expect this because if Nagel is serious about 'subjectivity' and 'objectivity' being relative notions marking a polarity, and moreover a unilinear polarity in which the objective pole is approached by progressively abstracting from the subjective pole, then he must accept that the two concepts are internally related; neither can be understood without reference to the other, and therefore there can be no applications of objectivity concepts which are nonrelatively valid. There is of course a need to assume that, for certain kinds of things, there is something they must be like in themselves, and that with respect to most things we must often and as far as possible prescind from particularities in our representations of them; but this speaks to what is convenient for us – for subjectivity, with its conceptual needs – a matter quite different from showing that realist claims about the knowledge-independent existence of certain entities are literally true. It is indeed hard to see why the former should be thought to imply anything about the latter. If, as Nagel says, the 'only solution' to the problem posed by the ineliminability of subjectivity is to think that ours is not a single world, or that there is no single way the world is in itself, then a very high price is being paid for not accepting that any account of the world must be essentially perspectival, which is the fact of epistemic life that the anti-realist seeks to get us to acknowledge.

But Nagel does not accept the anti-realist implications of his remarks, and offers instead an argument for the intelligibility of

---

28 *Ibid.*, pp. 210–211.
29 *Ibid.*
30 *Ibid.*
31 *Ibid.*, p. 213.

realist claims about the existence of entities beyond the possibilities of our ken. It is a two-chapter story like McGinn's. 'It certainly seems', Nagel says, 'that I can believe that reality extends beyond the reach of possible human thought, since this would be closely analogous to something which is not only possible but actually the case.'[32] The analogy is as follows (the examples are Nagel's). People blind from birth cannot conceive of colours. People with a permanent mental age of nine cannot understand Maxwell's equations. If all those who can understand colours and Maxwell's equations did not exist, but those blind nine-year-olds did, then there would be things to which they could not have cognitive access. Now the story elaborates somewhat: we are to imagine a world occupied jointly by ourselves and a race of higher beings, related to us as we are to the blind nine-year-olds. The higher beings accordingly comprehend what we cannot. Next, imagine that we occupy just such a world – only there are no such higher beings. 'Then what they could say if they did exist remains true. So it appears that the existence of unreachable aspects of reality is independent of their conceivability by any actual mind.'[33]

The second sentence of the two just quoted does not follow from the first. In the first it is counterfactually hypothesised that there might be aspects of reality reachable by higher beings. This neither entails the weaker thesis that there are in fact aspects of reality that current actual minds cannot reach, nor the stronger thesis that there are aspects of reality unreachable by any mind. Indeed this stronger thesis is ruled out by the terms of Nagel's hypothesis, which crucially requires accessibility to appropriate minds. Nagel takes himself to be saying (A) 'if there were things cognitively accessible to higher beings, then, even if we grant that there are no such higher beings, it still makes sense to think that those things exist'.[34] But he is actually saying something different, namely (B) 'if there were higher beings, then there could be things to which they but not we have cognitive access'; more

---

32 Nagel, *The View From Nowhere*, p. 95.
33 *Ibid.*, pp. 95–96.
34 This is weaker, and it does not require the simultaneous appeal to and dismissal of the higher beings.

explicitly still, 'if there were higher beings, then: possibly, there might be things to which they but not we have access'. The consequent states a possibility itself contingent on the counterfactual antecedent. From this there is nothing to be inferred about the possibility of conception-independent existence of given entities in general. The sense of the complex counterfactual itself turns precisely upon the possibility of a superior means of conception so that an assertion about the existence of the things in question can make sense; so it is not conception-independent existence we are talking about anyway.

To unravel this argument we must note the following. In (A) what is at stake is the possibility that things exist, in (B) it is the possibility that higher beings exist with powers superior to ours. Since Nagel is attempting to show that claims like (A) are intelligible, and since the story told in (B) is what he hopes will show that they are intelligible, (B) bears the burden of the argument. But for (B) to make (A) intelligible, we must make (B) intelligible; we must make sense of two things: first, the idea of higher beings who, secondly, conceive of higher things than can be conceived or known by us. The intelligibility of (B) is supposed to rest on the fact of there being actual blind nine-year-olds with respect to whom actual normal adults are cognitively superior. Now: how does the existence of blind nine-year-olds, and the gap between them and normal adults, make the thought of higher beings, and their higher knowledge, intelligible? Well – we (presumably) 'extrapolate'. We imagine ourselves to be blind nine-year-olds, and simultaneously we know what it is to be normal adults, and therefore we grasp the difference. Somehow we are to effect the 'extrapolation' by grasping (the same?) contrast between ourselves as normal adults and the imagined higher beings. But the move is spurious. To see why, compare the following case: 'we understand the contrast between the perceptual powers of a blind person and a sighted person. Therefore we understand the contrast between the perceptual powers of any normally endowed human and a being with a sixth (seventh, eighth) physical sensory modality unlike any of the standard human five.' Clearly, we do no such thing; and for the like reason, (B) is not made intelligible by the supposed comparison between normal adults and nine-year-olds.

But let us grant for a moment that the first part of (B), concerning the notion of beings with respect to whom we are like blind nine-year-olds, is rendered intelligible by this means. How does the possibility of such higher beings make intelligible the possibility of there being higher knowledge than we are in principle capable of grasping? It is already a prodigious feat to claim to know or to be able to conceive that there is something (from our point of view) unknowable or inconceivable, since it is unclear what licenses such a claim; but in advance of making it we should have to ponder the grounds for saying that if there were higher beings, then it is not merely that these beings would know more thoroughly, accurately or clearly what we do or can know, or what we do not yet know but will know; but that they would know more than it is possible for us to know. How can we know or conceive of that fact about them, given that *ex hypothesi* we do not know and are not able to know or conceive of what they can know? How are we in any position to say anything about their states of knowledge?

Once again, let us grant for a moment that it does make sense to claim in this way to know or to conceive that there is something unknowable or inconceivable from our point of view. Still, one has to note that it remains knowledge *from some point of view* which is at stake, and hence that it is not 'the existence of independent aspects of reality unreachable by any mind' which is being made intelligible. But this of course is what Nagel thinks he is making intelligible, for this is the import of (A). So even if we grant what we have no grounds for granting in respect of the intelligibility of (B), Nagel's argument fails.

It is possible to see a deeper reason for the failure of the McGinn and Nagel defences of realism in their not recognising that the 'absolute conception' has a status in our thought which renders it an entirely inappropriate topic for debate about whether or not it is true. It is crucial to realism that it be regarded as true, and the arguments just discussed are aimed at defending the plausibility, at very least, of asserting its truth. But once one sees the absolute conception as a special kind of assumption in our ordinary thinking and talking – a first-order assumption – one sees that the question of its truth or falsity does not and cannot arise at that level, nor at the second-order level of critical reflection on our epistemic practice, where the question does not concern the truth or falsity of the first-order realist assumption, but its role.[35] The point can be better appreciated, and the style of argument employed by McGinn and Nagel better understood, if we inspect a third attempt at the same style of defence of realism, one this time offered by Ian McFetridge.

The claim that how things are in the world is independent of the existence or character of knowing subjects – the fundamental realist claim – can, says McFetridge, be encapsulated in the schema, call it (R): 'It could be that p even though no human being or knowing subject knows, or could know, that p.'[36] McFetridge takes it that what the anti-realist asserts in opposition to this is that 'if p, then it could be known (by a human being or subject of experience) that p'.

The argument that instances of the schema (R) are assertible by realists, and so strongly that in McFetridge's view the corresponding anti-realism is rendered untenable, proceeds as follows. We know enough about ourselves and the natural world, says McFetridge, and in particular about how we acquire knowledge of the world, to make (R) 'overwhelmingly plausible'. What we know in particular is that there is nothing about the world and ourselves which 'guarantees that we must, in general, have the capacity to determine how things are in the world'.[37] He gives as an example the historical case. We can acquire knowledge of past events only if their causal descendants are sufficient, and sufficiently transparent, to make them accessible to us. 'And we know that such causal descendants are, given how the world is, sadly vulnerable to irrecoverable elimination. We know, therefore, that it is perfectly possible that, for example, the Venerable Bede should have died on such-and-such a day even though things are now such that nothing remains on the basis of which we could determine this.'[38]

---

35 See my 'Epistemology and Realism', *Proceedings of the Aristotelian Society* 1991.

36 McFetridge, I. G., 'Realism and Anti-realism in an Historical Context', in *Logical Necessity and other Essays*, Aristotelian Society Series, Vol. 11 (1990), p. 114.

37 *Ibid.*, p. 115.

38 *Ibid.*

From these thoughts McFetridge draws two conclusions. The first is that 'we have knowledge of the world and of our own modes of cognitive access to it which enables us to see, in many cases, not merely that the realist possibility of epistemic inaccessibility is an abstract philosophical possibility, but also how and why it is repeatedly realised'.[39]

McFetridge's second conclusion is that 'given the entrenchment' of realism in our ordinary view of ourselves and the world, it 'seems to be a *reductio ad absurdam* of any philosophy if it ends up simply denying' it. Instances of (R) 'could only be denied by one who was prepared and able to reconstruct our current common-sense-cum-scientific accounts of the world which seem to explain why, and hence justify the claim that, the present version of realism is, in many cases, true'.[40]

Note first that McFetridge begins by characterising the realist claim in terms of its being possible that p is the case even if it is impossible for p to be known. The difficulty with this claim is obvious: how can it itself be known or at very least be made to seem plausible, given that on its own terms everything is *ex hypothesi* ruled out as supporting the embedded claim 'p is the case'? As with McGinn and Nagel, McFetridge seeks to make (R) plausible by giving us an example of an actual such case, for then (R) is justified *ab esse ad posse*. The case he offers is of historical facts lost to view – specifically, the Venerable Bede's date of death, unknown and now impossible to discover but about which there is of course some fact of the matter. But 'lost' historical facts are an obviously poor example: the date of the Venerable Bede's death is not something that 'no knowing subject could know'; on the contrary, its being (presently) unknown is a merely contingent matter. The date of Bede's death was once known, and if certain contingencies had held could now be known, and for all we know might yet be ascertained. So historical examples do not help. The question is, could any example help? It seems not, for *per impossibile* what would have to be shown is that something is the case which it is impossible to know to be so.

---

39 *Ibid.*
40 *Ibid.*

McFetridge's way of characterising opposition to (R) fails to convey its point. The anti-realist's demand is that claims about something's being the case should be non-arbitrary, which is to say, motivated and supported. To satisfy this demand something must count as a ground on which p can be asserted. The demand can be represented as embodying a condition on the sense of the expression used to assert p: if nothing so counts, no assertion is being made; language is idling.

The chief interest in McFetridge's argument lies in its detail. We know enough, says McFetridge, to make (R) 'overwhelmingly plausible'. What we know in particular is that the world outruns our capacities to investigate it. McFetridge describes this view as 'entrenched' in our ordinary conception of ourselves, the world, and the relation between them, in such a way that denying it would, as noted, constitute a *reductio ad absurdam* of the view that led to that denial. He does, however, allow that such a denial is possible for anyone prepared 'to reconstruct our current common-sense-cum-scientific accounts of the world which serve to explain why, and hence to justify the claim that, the present version of realism is, in many cases, true'. A little reflection shows that a familiar mistake is at work here. It is that an *assumption* of a given conceptual scheme, as McFetridge effectively acknowledges it is, is in fact or also something besides: namely, a *truth revealed by* that conceptual scheme. Here the realist commitment to the independence of the world from knowledge or experience of it is a constitutive feature of our 'current common-sense-cum-scientific' account of the world. It is an assumption we premise in order to go on to give, in terms of the account resting on it, the familiar story about our causal relations with the world, to which our theories assign properties – for prime examples, spatial and temporal dimensions – which transcend our investigative powers, because the practical value of doing so is high. The common mistake is to think that because the theories based on this assumption have such great utility, the assumption itself is thereby shown to be true. To pretheoretical reflection it may seem natural to suppose that a theory which works is true, given suitable criteria for what the theory's working consists in; but the supposition is of course mistaken. Ptolemaic astronomy 'works' for a wide range of purposes – navigating the seas, predicting eclipses – but we would not suppose this to entail its truth. The point is entirely general and familiar: nothing derived from an assumption employed as a premise in that derivation can, without circularity, prove the truth of the assumption itself.

McFetridge's account makes it plain that the style of argument advanced by him and the others discussed here has as its ambition the goal of showing that the realist assumption is *true*. What is shown by counters to this style of argument is that its ambition is misplaced. The realist assumption is precisely that: an assumption, and the real task is not to try to prove it true, but to understand the work it does in serving as a strategic commitment in thought.

Reflection on the two-chapter arguments of Nagel and McGinn in the light of these remarks about McFetridge suggests that there is a certain pattern to realist efforts at making intelligible the claim that realism is true. The simplest illustration of it is the notion that one can conceive of the world without any form of sentience, still less thought, present in it. One imagines the trees and grass bathed in sunlight and blowing in the breeze; and then one abstracts oneself and all other sentient perspectives from the picture (from the picture, one notes in passing; but nothing turns on the imagism of the image) as if this amounted to grasping how things would be independently of any perspective. The speciousness of this manoeuvre, and it is the same manoeuvre that underlies Nagel's juggling with introduced and eliminated perspectives in the higher-beings story earlier recounted, would have long since been plain if the argument of Berkeley's *Principles* section 23 had not been so casually expressed by him and so woefully misunderstood by his commentators.[41] That insight is the simple one that nothing can be said or thought about anything which is not conditioned by that talk or thought of it; and hence that there is no account to be given of any realm of entities, or indeed any subject-matter, which does not essentially involve whatever makes the giving of that account itself possible. This, restated, is the anti-realist case.

Sometimes Nagel writes as though his version of the two-chapter story aims to support only a weak pro-realist stance: 'My position is that realism makes as much sense as many other unverifi-

---

41 See my *Berkeley: The Central Questions* (London, 1986), pp. 113–117.

able statements, even though all of them, and all thought, may present fundamental philosophical mysteries to which there is at present no solution.'[42] But at other times Nagel makes more strongly pro-realist remarks. We cannot dispense, he says, with 'a robust sense of reality and its independence of any form of human understanding' – which he asserts just one page after stating that 'appearance and perspective are essential parts of what there is'.[43] There is a strong taste here of a cake being eaten and had – but only if the claims constitutive of the 'robust sense' are asserted to be true, as opposed to being undischargeable assumptions of the scheme that creatures cognitively organised like us must (the modality is important: that is what makes the assumption undischargeable) make.

This observation prompts a closing thought. McGinn and Nagel each insist that we both desire and need a full-blooded realist metaphysics. In his *Mind* paper McGinn says: 'We need to cultivate a vision of reality (a metaphysics) that makes it truly independent of our given cognitive powers.' In *The Subjective View* he says: 'we wish a conception of physical objects as existentially independent of us – a conception that permits us to say "if no perceivers had existed, physical objects still would (or could) have".' Nagel locates the source of much philosophical error in an 'insufficiently robust sense of reality'. Now, most self-respecting anti-realists would find little to quarrel with in such assertions, if they describe the strategic assumptions of our conceptual scheme. But of course both mean that it makes sense to treat assertions of the existence of the cognitively inaccessible as literally true; that reality must be 'really real' in the sense required by the independence thesis; that it is reality thus transcendently conceived that we need and desire.

Why should we accept this? Realism so conceived generates epistemological scepticism, by forcing a gap between the world and cognition of it which prompts intractable difficulties about how representation of the world can provide representers with adequate grounds for beliefs about it. Realism so conceived also makes the matter of how we acquire and employ our discourse

---

42 Nagel, *The View From Nowhere*, p. 95.
43 *Ibid.*, pp. 5, 4, respectively.

about the world – our thought and talk – mysterious. How do we come to think as we do, and to master a language, if much or indeed most of what our discourse ranges over putatively lies beyond our capacities to cognise it?

These are familiar points. The present point is this: if anti-Realism is to be refuted, or equivalently, if the intelligibility of the realist's transcendent, epistemologically-unconstrained meta-physical claims are to be demonstrated, arguments different from those considered here are needed.

10
Evidence and judgment

In the clear atmosphere of theoretical abstraction the aim of enquiry tends to be something neat: a sealed and guaranteed account of truth, knowledge, consciousness, or whatever concept or property lies under investigation. At the same time we are sharply aware that practical life is a messier business, and the standards employed are by no means so exigent, because we cannot afford the luxury of demanding that they should be. There are plenty of cases where, for example, hard moral decisions have to be taken on the basis of incomplete data and seemingly incompletable theorising: some fatal decision on a hospital ward, say. Of course philosophers have responded to this fact by focusing attention on the apparatuses required: practical reasoning, decision and probability theories and complementary areas of epistemology and epistemic logic provide good cases in point. Nor are the *pure* as opposed to explicitly *applied* areas of philosophical theory irrelevant: counsels of perfection and hermetic definitions can work like the reference grid-lines on a map, potent aids in difficult terrain.

The relationship between abstract speculation and the business of living is not, of course, a one-way street. The latter not only prompts but illuminates the former. So, as we would expect, a difference can be made to our reflections on, say, the nature of the justification of belief and the operation of our conceptual scheme, by paying attention to what we do in practice when our practice particularly matters. In what follows I indicate (in an informal and simplified way) an area of epistemic practice which, when reflected upon, offers enrichment to our appreciation of some central concerns in epistemology. It happens that the practice in question is itself of great intrinsic importance, and has received detailed exploration at the hands of experts, which I do not seek to recapitulate or engage with here; my aim lies elsewhere. Here some preliminaries only are sketched, to take from them certain suggestions for general epistemic practice.

The area in question is the task which a jury has to perform at the end of criminal proceedings in a court of law (as constituted in the common law tradition). Put crudely – as we shall quickly see, too crudely – the jury has to decide whether the accused is guilty or not of the offence with which he has been charged. In criminal proceedings (of sufficient seriousness to warrant trial before a jury) a person is brought before a court, where by 'court' is understood a properly constituted body typically consisting of (a) a judge or judges, (b) a jury, picked at random from those on the electoral role of adult age (until the early 1970s in England there were property and income qualifications for jury service: one criterion was that only an occupant of a dwelling having at least 15 windows was allowed to serve) and subject to challenge for suitability, (c) people learned in the law and licensed to plead at the bar of the court on behalf of the parties, *viz.* counsel for the prosecution and for the defendant.

The point of the proceedings is to 'try the case' which the prosecution adduces in support of the indictment specifying the charge against the defendant. Note this fact: it is strictly speaking the *case* which is tried, not the *defendant* who is tried. The defendant is presumed innocent, a vital protection of individual liberty against summary authority, and a vital ingredient in the 'due process' which is essential to fair and proper proceedings. This point is vital to understanding the epistemic task that the jury faces in the course of the trial. In one sense it has to ignore the person against whom a charge has been laid, and concentrate on the case brought by the prosecution in its attempt to prove the charge, in a sense of 'prove' shortly to be examined. The court's job overall is to decide on the merits of that case. It is the judge's sole responsibility to do so with respect to law (usually a pretty straightforward matter in criminal cases; civil law is much more interesting; but the judge's role in, for example, deciding what is admissible in evidence is particularly important), and it is the jury's responsibility to do so with respect to questions of fact. In criminal proceedings the questions of fact are of course central.

The crucial question is: what exactly is the jury being asked to decide? One might think that the answer is obvious enough and has already been given: namely, that it must decide whether or not the defendant is guilty as charged. But if one examines the premises of the proceedings and the specific tasks which the prosecution and defence have in hand, one sees that this is not strictly speaking so. A good way of identifying the jury's task is to look at what the prosecution is trying to get the jury to think, and what the defence is trying to do in response. First, remember that the defendant is presumed to be innocent. Bentham pointed out that this is a fiction, and indeed an absurd one, since if the defendant were genuinely presumed innocent he would not have been arrested in the first place. But the presumption of innocence is of vital theoretical importance to the proceedings, because it not only places the burden of proof on the prosecution – in theory, the burden lies *entirely* with the prosecution (*in practice* the defence has a burden too) – but it does so in a particular way. This is that the target of the prosecution's efforts is getting the jury into a *state of mind* in which they feel they *should*, on considerations of *reasonableness*, take the *evidence* offered as a ground for *abandoning the presumption* they make as to the defendant's innocence. There are five closely connected points in what has just here been said, each demanding attention. In order to appreciate the full import of this characterisation of the prosecution's task, note this: a 'not guilty' verdict is an odd thing to call a not guilty verdict, because *technically* the jury is not faced with an open question; the situation is not technically one in which the defendant's guilt or innocence is undecided and in the balance, so that the jury have to come down one side or other of that balance. The defendant is presumed innocent all along, so the prosecution case must not merely tip a balance, but overturn a *status quo*. Therefore if the jury returns a 'not guilty' verdict, what it is strictly saying is that it has *not been persuaded* to upset that *status quo*, that is, to abandon its presumption of the defendant's innocence. The question of whether the defendant *is in fact* innocent is not the point; the jury was not asked, 'here is an innocent man; is he innocent?' but 'here is an innocent man; and here is a case – evidence and argument – which has it that it is unreasonable to continue thinking him so; are you persuaded by that case?' Strictly, therefore, the jury's task is one of judging the prosecution's case, that is, whether that case is proved or not. And they do this by seeing whether they are persuaded by it.

We can immediately notice, therefore, that a case might be 'proved' in the sense at issue, that is, it might not be reasonable not to accept it, quite independently of whether or not in fact the defendant did what he is alleged to have done. So, a guilty man might be let off because the prosecution did not prepare and present a good enough case to persuade the jury; and an innocent man might go to prison because, let us say, so-called evidence undetectably fabricated by the police is so strong in its probative character that the jury, trusting it and its source and thus assuming that the required *ceteris paribus* clause operates, would not be acting reasonably if they rejected it.

So, the jury's task turns out to be to decide whether they are persuaded by the prosecution's case to abandon their presumption in favour of the defendant's innocence. It is a further inference from this decision to the proposition that the defendant is guilty; and it is by no means a secure inference, since the fact that the jury is convinced by the prosecution case by no means entails the defendant's guilt, as just noted. It is this consideration which Plato exploits in the *Theaetetus*, where Socrates considers the point that a jury might be convinced by the persuasive powers and rhetorical devices of a skilful lawyer to hold someone guilty, independently of whether or not he is truly so. The example is meant to illustrate the difference between true belief and knowledge, because in the *Theaetetus* example the accused is indeed guilty, so the lawyer's rhetoric has induced a true belief in the jurors' minds; but it does not count as knowledge for Plato, for the familiar reasons. But the chief point is obvious enough: the aim of the prosecution's endeavours is to persuade the jury of the defendant's guilt, which as we see is not the same thing as establishing the defendant's guilt. (There is meant to be a check on this in the conception of the prosecutor as *amicus curiae*; he cannot go 'all out' for a conviction, unlike the defence which can go all out for an acquittal; the prosecutor must, so the piety goes, above all serve the truth. But this does not alter the fact that the aim of his endeavours has to be to get the jury to believe something in a certain way – namely, strongly enough – to justify the charge which he, the prosecutor, lays against the defendant.) So – the prosecution's aim is not to establish the defendant's guilt, but to persuade the jury of the defendant's guilt; that is, the aim is to produce a certain state of mind in the jury, one which we might for the moment loosely characterise as 'being sure' or 'being convinced' that it is unreasonable to continue regarding the defendant as innocent.

Once matters have been put in this light it is easy to characterise the defence's task: which is to subvert the prosecution's effort to persuade the jury into the state of mind in question. It is relatively speaking a much easier task than the one facing the prosecution, because all the defence need do in order to get the jury to conclude that they are unpersuaded by the prosecution's case, is to leave enough doubt in their minds as to whether what the prosecution brings forward in evidence and argument is enough to overturn their presumption in favour of the defendant's innocence. (Once again, we note that this is quite independent of what the truth might be, for it is not what is the case but what can most reasonably be taken to be the case which is at issue.)

We come therefore to the philosophically problematic aspects of the picture thus drawn. They concern the five points emphasised in the description of the prosecution's task earlier described: 'the target of the prosecution's efforts is getting the jury into a *state of mind* in which they feel they *should*, on considerations of *reasonableness*, take the *evidence* offered as a ground for *abandoning the presumption* they make as to the defendant's innocence.' These points are too closely connected to be taken independently, but it is revealing to consider them in two stages. I begin with the first three points, which together concern the question of the attitude the prosecution seeks to persuade the jury into, on grounds of reasonableness, to their presumption of the defendant's innocence; and then I go on to consider the complex question of evidence, which as we shall see makes a substantial difference to our understanding of the question.

The starting-point is the prosecution's designs on each juror's psychological state. It is not helpful to describe this target state simply as an epistemic state, nor even as a particular kind of epistemic state, namely a doxastic state (a state of belief) – although the target is of course fundamentally this, for the jurors will have been induced by the prosecution to believe one or more things which can be represented propositionally among the reasons they have for sustaining or relinquishing their presumption of the defendant's innocence. Rather, the state is one which might best be described as an *adverbial attitude*; for it is not just that the jurors have to believe something, but they have to do so in a certain manner; they have to believe *strongly enough* to abandon the innocence presumption. For a juror might believe the defendant guilty, but also feel that the prosecution case has gaps in it, and therefore not believe strongly enough to convict, since doubt remains. Not any doubt will do; the formula has it that such doubt must be 'reasonable'. Since this notorious conception comes so immediately to the fore, something must be said about it now before the state-of-mind question can be further analysed. (Other and further points relating to reasonable doubt emerge later.)

The phrase 'reasonable doubt' is a key one in criminal proceedings; it is standardly used by judges and counsel in their admonitions to juries on their duties. They tell jurors that in civil cases decisions are reached on the balance of probabilities, but in criminal cases a much more demanding standard is set: no reasonable doubt must remain in jurors' minds if they are to convict.

The phrase is as vague as it is important. It has often been the subject of attempts at working definitions taking this characteristically circular form: proof beyond reasonable doubt is proof which a reasonable man or woman would accept as settling doubt. If doubt remains in the face of the case offered, it must not be fanciful or imagined doubt, nor doubt concocted by a juror in order to avoid an unpleasant duty. A proposition established 'beyond reasonable doubt' is therefore one as to which the jury has to be 'sure' or 'fully satisfied' or 'entirely convinced' or 'satisfied to a moral certainty'. Here I am using the phraseology of judges' quoted directions on the matter.

It is not hard to see that these working definitions are, even when not circular, very imprecise. Only one thing is immediately clear: by 'proof' is meant roughly what Hume had in mind in using this expression; it is not demonstrative or conclusive proof as we think of it in connexion with valid and sound deductions in a formal system; it is something less in probative force and different in logical kind, which nevertheless commands assent and directs action, and does so in such a way that to dissent, or to act contrary to that direction, would count as unreasonable. And obviously enough this shows that in specifying the kind of non-demonstrative proof at issue, part of the nub of the problem is going to lie with the conception of what is 'reasonable'. In practice courts do not have time for refined deliberations upon rationality and the ethics of rationality, and so the test of reasonableness is standardly an external or *ad hoc* one: it is the test of consensus, that is, of what most normal people would regard as settling doubt or as furnishing a strong enough ground for choosing or acting in one way rather than another. It is customary to find, in legal proceedings, appeal being made to common sense, to what the majority, or the ordinary man or woman in the street, would think or feel, as a way of settling what is reasonable. (An allied resource is central to the law on obscenity, for example.) As is well known, this is a fallacy in informal logic – the general appeal to what most people believe is a fallacy of relevance. The standard defence is to say that it is not clear what alternative practical and general test there can be for the required notion of 'reasonable-ness'; we are bound to rely on it, at the same time hoping that ways can be found of tightening the slack in the notion in the particular circumstances of particular cases; precisely one of our expectations of defence counsel is that they will be competent to do just that.

If that is all there is to the 'reasonableness' question, there appears to be considerable room for unease; for there is another serious difficulty here too, which can be illustrated by reminding ourselves of a problem with Cartesian epistemology. Descartes claimed that his aim in the *Meditations* was to attain epistemo-logical 'certainty'. Now certainty is a psychological state, and being in this state does not make true, nor does it necessarily mark as true, the beliefs one entertains while in it. So I might be certain that Red Rum will win the next Derby, or be certain that astrological categories accurately describe human types, and be wrong. It was precisely Descartes' tactic to make 'a feeling of certainty that p' a guarantee of the truth of p; a feeling of certainty generated by a certain procedure is a mark of truth because there is a deity who is good; a good deity would not wish us to be deceived when by careful means we have come to feel certain that

p, and therefore feeling certain that p (under the suitable methodological constraints and divine dispositions) settles that p is true.
Other considerations apart, Descartes' approach vividly illustrates
what is wrong with making a state of mind such as certainty or
conviction the aim of epistemic proceedings, rather than a detachable concomitant of the aim: for the ideal must surely be that one
should arrive at the truth or the best justification for a given belief,
not at a frame of mind you could be in when believing falsehoods.

As noted, the prosecution tries to induce a state of mind in jurors
like the one Descartes sought; not of course on the basis that a
deity guarantees that this state of mind does the epistemic trick,
but, seemingly not much more satisfactorily, on the basis of what
might be supposed 'reasonable'.

Put like this, the epistemology of what is expected of a jury
does not look good; but this is not all there is to the matter, for
we have not yet considered the question of evidence and probative value, and we have not tested alternative ways of articulating
the thought that reasonableness is the right criterion given the
constraints of practice within whose limits we are working. And
as we would expect, once we have taken the question of evidence
into account, the picture does indeed look different.

There is in legal theorising about evidence recognition of the risk
posed by the fact that what the prosecution aims to arouse in
jurors is a subjective adverbial attitude, namely belief which persuasion has induced them to hold strongly enough to abandon
the innocence presumption. One can illustrate this particularly
well by considering Bentham's seminal contribution to the debate
about evidence (*The Rationale of Judicial Evidence*, 1827). First,
however, it is necessary to note certain distinctions. 'Evidence' is
a catholic concept which embraces importantly different subspecies. On Bentham's definition it is 'any matter of fact, the effect,
tendency, or design of which, when presented to the mind, is to
produce a persuasion concerning the existence of some other fact;
a persuasion either affirmative or disaffirmative of its existence'.
The relation between the *factum probans* and the *factum proban-
dum* is at least one of relevance; the question of what more is
sufficient for the former to serve as evidence for the latter in part
turns on the question whether, as I suggest above and Bentham

suggests here, it is right to see the aim of bringing evidence forward as the subjective psychological one of producing specified adverbial attitudes in jurors' minds. The subspecies of evidence which is central in criminal proceedings is *testimony*. Of course so-called 'real evidence', namely, objects like the jemmy, swagbag, striped jersey and little black mask of the burglar, is exhibited in court; but all such evidence, in Bentham's view, is circumstantial evidence only: it is founded on 'analogy [and] the relation of cause and effect', and so its probative value is similar to secondhand information or any evidence which is for one reason or another indirect or inferential in ways which contrast with the directness of, for example, eye-witness testimony. But testimony is the primary focus of interest, and it may be defined as evidence provided by persons.[1] The notion of testimony itself admits of division, most usefully into two broad categories: formal and informal testimony, the first kind being the sort which is produced on oath or affirmation in a court of law, the latter being the sort which we all provide for one another in the course of everyday life.[2] Coady argues that informal testimony is a central epistemic resource in our conceptual scheme, an argument aimed at contesting the Cartesian ideal of 'autonomous knowledge' as the target of enquiry. The role of informal testimony is important in the vexed matter of the reasonableness of belief, as we shall see upon returning to that question shortly; indeed the importance of the claim that testimony is a source of knowledge is well illustrated by the debate on it: the view has been attacked by some (for example, Collingwood, who argued that it cannot be relied upon in historical research because of its subjectivity and the often insurmountable difficulties in securing independent verification for it) and regarded as central by others (for example, Thomas Reid; and Coady himself).

Bentham took it to be vitally necessary that the sources of trustworthiness and untrustworthiness in testimony should be identified, and steps taken to limit the latter by the provision of 'securities', some of them procedural, that is, embodied in the

---

1 C. A. J. Coady, *Testimony: A Philosophical Study* (1992).
2 *Ibid.*, p. 27.

very nature of a court's method of conducting its business. He characterised the main risks to the trustworthiness of testimony as arising from mendacity, incorrectness, incompleteness and indistinctness. The steps required to avoid these dangers are heterogeneous: suitable sanctions have to be available to prevent mendacity, such as the employment of oath, punishment, and shame; and there have to be appropriate procedures to ensure completeness and correctness of the testimony given by witnesses, for example by ensuring that it is particular, subjected to test by interrogation, and expressed distinctly and in permanent form (i.e. a written record should be kept of it). Also the courts must have power to get the information they require, and the whole proceedings must be public – in Bentham's view publicity is the key to giving 'power and efficiency to all the other instruments'. It is interesting that Bentham thought that it is not the jury which is the glory of the English legal system, but public trial by oral examination and cross-examination, as providing the best conceivable opportunity for getting and weighing evidence.

Now, if we understand testifying as the offering of evidence by given persons in support of some proposition, we immediately note that if we think of it as a certain type of speech act we can identify certain features of it which are particularly relevant to the question at issue ('what is the jury's task?'). On Austin's view (*How To Do Things With Words*, p. 161) to describe testifying as an illocutionary act performed with specific intentions in certain conditions enables us to specify the conventions constitutive of it. (Austin calls testimony 'expositive' like swearing, reporting, conjecturing.) As suggested by Coady [3] these conventions are as follows: a speaker testifies by making a statement that p if he has a relevant competence to offer p in evidence for some unresolved question; p is such evidence; and the testifier offers it to someone in need of such evidence. Although testifying of course counts among the illocutionary acts aimed at giving an audience information, it has a distinctive property: the property of being offered by one who, on that occasion or in that respect, is an especially qualified source. Someone is a provider of testimony, in other

---

3 *Ibid.*, p. 42.

words, because he is in some sort of privileged position as regards the information he conveys. The fact that someone's being a testifier involves his making this claim about his authority with respect to the content of the testimony, figures centrally in his intentions in performing the act of testifying, and this is understood by his audience; who therefore have an opportunity, if they can be satisfied that a *ceteris paribus* clause operates (he is honest, etc.), to treat the information thus conveyed as true; that is, they can treat the testimony as a source of knowledge. Of course, someone's testifying is logically no better than someone's reading words from a piece of paper in a language he does not understand, so far as an entailment to the truth of what is said goes; testifiers can be lying or deceiving, or unwittingly be possessed of false information. But in the standard case the conditions on testimony select it as a species of information-conveying which is intended to have just such a high probative value. In particular, it is not the expression of opinion, it is not fiction, it is not hypothesising: it is meant to be the conveying of information pure and simple.

This is made abundantly clear in the case of formal testimony. Among the securities identified as necessary is the refusal to take hearsay evidence as testimony, and the controls placed on the admissibility of 'expert witnesses'. The aim of these restrictions is to put the jury into the best possible situation for an assessment of the probative value of the testimony offered. The witness has been selected for his standing in the case, he has been sworn and is liable to sanctions if he lies, he is allowed only to report what he has proper warrant to report, his evidence is elicited by inter-rogation and subjected to the scrutiny of cross-interrogation, and what he says is subsequently weighed in conjunction with, and comparison to, other evidence offered. Given these and allied safeguards, as much has been done as is possible to allow the jury to judge whether or not to accept the evidence offered as having sufficient probative force to induce in them the crucial change of mind about the defendant's innocence.

I use the expression 'probative force' advisedly, rather than 'truth': it is not strictly speaking open to the jury to decide whether what a witness says is true, but it is open to them to decide how much credence to give it. The threshold degree of credence, as I earlier characterised it, which they accord to testi-

mony and other evidence, is precisely the trigger of their preparedness to change their minds in the crucial respect.

There is no question but that in practice jurors often take
themselves to be accepting certain claims as true and others as
false, just as no doubt they represent their task to themselves as
literally deciding between innocence and guilt. But the epistemic
character of the assessment of testimony cannot be understood
properly in that light. This is quickly illustrated by the fact that
the test of 'reasonableness' in assessment of evidence would be
the wrong one if what the jury was chiefly concerned with were
cut and dried: to refuse to accept something recognised as true is
not unreasonable but insane. Nor, however, is it altogether helpful, although in one sense it is correct, to describe the jury's task
in terms of a calculation of probabilities, because apart from
the fact that it is not a *balance* of probabilities they are trying to
determine, their situation is not one of calibrating a degree of
likelihood, but entirely one of asking whether the evidence has a
degree of likelihood, whatever it is, above a certain limit, in virtue
of which it will trigger a change of mind: as if it is a certain kind
of epistemic threshold that alone matters. And indeed this suggests that there is something right in Bentham's remarks about
what came to be called 'the thermometer of persuasion', namely,
the degree of probative force which would prompt an ordinary
person to lay a wager or take out insurance. He writes: '[The]
various degrees of which belief is susceptible, have a very strong
influence on our conduct; it would be more correct to say that all
our determinations depend upon them. We have an obvious
application of them in wagers [and] insurances ... If different
degrees of conjectural strength in wagers and insurances can be
expressed, why should it not be possible to express likewise the
different proving power in testimony?' Notoriously, Bentham
suggested scales of 0 to 10 for persuasion, one each for affirmative and negative persuasion, with zero 'denoting the absence of
all belief either for or against the fact in question'; and witnesses
in court were to assign a value to what they said. The jury need
only do some simple arithmetic to come to a determination.

Although this clearly will not do, there is something right in it,
something quite familiar and unexceptionable; namely, that a
degree of persuasion less than absolute certainty triggers decision

and action in daily life. What it is germane to note is that one neither does nor needs to go into numbers to determine what it is; but whatever it is it will be supported by a conjunction of what Aristotle calls the 'endoxa', the commonly held beliefs of mankind, and the facts particular to the case. And this is what the jury relies upon when presented with the best evidence the system can offer them. It does not alter the fact that the aim of presenting them with the evidence in this way is to persuade them into a certain state of mind: but it does suggest that the system of criminal justice does itself an unnecessary disservice in one respect when it fails to provide a satisfying justification for the 'reasonableness' test with respect to doubt, because the apparently *ad hoc* appeal to what anybody might think about the case in hand is less *ad hoc* than it seems. No-one makes wagers or takes out insurance on general grounds; the degree of probative force evidence has for someone to wager or insure in a given manner depends entirely on the facts of the case, given the background of beliefs which interpret them. I am inclined to argue that the background beliefs themselves provide weightings for the particular case: even that the question whether the probative force of given evidence pushes it over the threshold triggering a change of belief is a matter that is in large part determined by them. In a court of law the standard is certainly no less than that employed in such cases, and it is arguably higher, since individuals in the course of ordinary epistemic practice might not be as well served as a jury is with evidence and with prepared opposing assessments of its source, nature and implications.

In this last sense a court of law might not be a mirror of life; but in all other crucial respects of epistemic assessment it is. Some of the lessons that might be drawn have a familiar ring. There is a model of our epistemic practices which describes us as having, with respect to contingent matters of fact, at best only defeasible warrant for the judgments we make, constituted by an assortment of constraints which we impose on the evidence we collect and the means we have of collecting it, the object being to ensure that it will be as well shrived as it can be before we act and choose in accordance with it. Suicide apart, there is no option to choosing on the basis of local and incomplete information, and our reliance on the 'endoxa' and these rough calibrations of the probative value of evidence acquired by sense-experience, memory and testimony, has therefore to be total. Moreover, the mental state we induce in ourselves by these means is an adverbial attitude, typically, belief which is something enough – strong enough, weak enough, or whatever – to justify the action or inaction which ensues. On this familiar model there is no room for a global sceptical attack on our epistemic practice; scepticism has always to be of the local, healthy sort which asks us whether believing some particular thing is genuinely reasonable, all things considered.

In theorising about law, jurisprudents do not, as far as one can gather from the literature, see a study of the logic of the jury's task as yielding a result which is so closely like one general model of epistemic practice. That it does so seems to me interesting and significant, not least because while clarifying what is happening in the jury case, itself of some help, it reinforces a broadly anti-realist epistemological view: for the jury considerations show that we are not working with a causal theory of knowledge, or a pre-supposed realism as to pre-existent (analogy: independently exist-ing) 'facts of the case': the jury does not uncover 'the facts' or determine truth or falsity; it decides whether on the evidence and arguments, *ceteris paribus*, it is persuaded to give up the presump-tion of innocence. And this is more or less how things are with us in the course of epistemic daily life.

Index